# EMERALD H

## A Modern Explorer's Guide to Ireland's Heart and Hidden Gems

Richard Wesley

Copyright © 2024 by Richard Wesley

All rights reserved. No part of this book may be reproduced, distributed, or transmitted in any form or by any means, including photocopying, recording, or other electronic or mechanical methods, without the prior written permission of the publisher, except in the case of brief quotations embodied in critical reviews and certain other noncommercial uses permitted by copyright law.

This book is intended for informational purposes only. While every effort has been made to ensure the accuracy of the information contained herein, the author and publisher assume no responsibility for errors or omissions, or for damages resulting from the use of the information contained herein.

# CONTENTS

INTRODUCTION ............................................................. 7

Welcome to Ireland ...................................................... 7

Navigating This Guide .................................................. 9

SETTING THE SCENE ................................................. 12

The Irish Landscape .................................................. 12

Understanding Irish Culture and Traditions ............. 16

ESSENTIAL TRAVEL TIPS ........................................ 19

Planning Your Journey: Best Times to Visit ............ 19

Getting There .............................................................. 23

Transport Options for Navigating Ireland ................ 25

Staying Connected in Ireland .................................... 28

Money Matters ............................................................ 31

THE MUST-SEE CITIES ............................................. 35

Dublin: The Heartbeat of Ireland ............................. 35

Historical Dublin Landmarks to Explore ................. 37

Pubs, Music, and Nightlife ........................................ 40

Dublin for Foodies ..................................................... 43

Cork: Gateway to the South ............... 46

The English Market and Beyond ............... 48

Exploring Kinsale and Cobh ............... 50

Galway: The Cultural Soul of Ireland ............... 53

Street Performers and Seafront Strolls ............... 54

THE GREAT OUTDOORS ............... 57

The Wild Atlantic Way ............... 57

The Cliffs of Moher ............... 60

Connemara ............... 62

Cycling in Ireland ............... 64

Best National Parks for Hiking ............... 67

Surfing and Sea Kayaking Hotspots ............... 71

Best Golf Courses ............... 73

OFF THE BEATEN PATH ............... 76

Hidden Villages to Explore ............... 76

Top Ancient Sites to Explore ............... 78

Best Island Hopping Spots ............... 81

CULTURAL IMMERSION ............... 84

Where to Experience Irish Music and Dance .... 84

Festivals Not to Miss ............... 87

ACCOMMODATIONS ............... 90

Castle Hotels for a Royal Stay ............... 90

Cozy Bed and Breakfasts ............... 93

Budget-Friendly Hostels and Camping ............ 96

FOOD AND DRINK ............... 99

Traditional Irish Dishes to Try ............... 99

The Craft Beer and Whiskey Scene ............ 101

SAFETY AND ETIQUETTE ............... 104

Navigating Ireland Safely ............... 104

Health Services for Tourists ............ 106

PLANNING YOUR DEPARTURE ............... 109

Souvenirs and Memories to Bring Back Home 109

Reflecting on Your Journey ............... 111

IRELAND ITINERARIES ................................................. 114

Weekend Getaway (2-3 Days) ........................ 114

Weeklong Adventure (6-7 days) ..................... 115

Two Weeks of Exploration .............................. 116

APPENDICES ................................................................ 118

Useful Phrases in Irish ..................................... 118

Useful Contacts and Resources ...................... 121

Irish Festivals Calendar .................................... 123

Travel Checklist ................................................ 126

# INTRODUCTION

Welcome to Ireland

Tucked away on the Atlantic coast, Ireland—sometimes called the Emerald Isle because of its emerald landscapes—is a place where legends and reality collide to create tapestry rich in natural beauty, history, and culture. It's a place where lively cities throb with the warmth and inventiveness of their citizens, and historic stone castles stand as silent testaments to the past. Immerse yourself in a land of dreams and stories in Ireland, where each stone, glen, and stream has a story to tell.

## The Whisper of History

It's like traveling through time when you walk through Ireland. There are countless tales from ancient times all around us, from the mysterious spirals of Newgrange to the sombre solitude of the Rock of Cashel. Not only are these historic locations older than the Egyptian pyramids, but they also serve as windows into a bygone era when druids and chieftains ruled and had close relationships with the natural world. Ireland's history speaks to you from its craggy landscapes and wind-tossed ruins, not just from books.

## A Landscape of Dreams

The natural splendor of Ireland is legendary. The 2,500 km long Wild Atlantic Way is a marvel of the strength and beauty of nature, with beaches that sparkle in the sun and cliffs that plunge into the thunderous ocean below. The wild beauty of Ireland's coast is embodied by the Cliffs of Moher, with their breathtaking drop into the Atlantic. On the other hand, a different kind of beauty that calms the spirit and piques the imagination is spoken of by the serene lakes of Killarney and the mysterious hills of Connemara.

## Navigating This Guide

"Emerald Horizons is intended to be more than a travel guide; it will accompany you as you explore Ireland's heart, providing insights into its history, culture, landscapes, and people. Whether you're a seasoned traveler or visiting the Emerald Isle for the first time, this guide aims to make your trip as enjoyable and memorable as possible. Here are some pointers to help you navigate this guide effectively and tailor your Irish adventure to your specific preferences and interests.

1. Embrace the Journey, Not Just the Destination

Ireland is a country where the journey is as interesting as the destinations themselves. Allow yourself to explore beyond the main attractions while following this guide. The suggested itineraries and hidden gems are intended to promote spontaneity and discovery. Allow the road to take you to unexpected places; it's often the small, unplanned experiences that leave the deepest impressions.

2. Engage with the Culture

This guide is filled with opportunities to delve deeply into Irish culture. Engaging with the culture, whether by learning a few phrases in Irish Gaelic or understanding the historical context of the places you visit, will significantly improve your experience. Attend local music events, participate in festivals, and don't be afraid to strike up conversations with locals. Irish warmth and hospitality are legendary, and interactions can provide insights that no guidebook can.

3. Respect and Preserve

As you explore Ireland's natural beauty and historical sites, remember how important it is to respect and preserve these treasures. This guide emphasizes sustainable travel practices, such as supporting local businesses and following Leave No Trace principles while outdoors. Your mindfulness ensures that these wonders continue to inspire travelers for generations to come.

4. Adapt and Be Flexible

Ireland's weather is well-known for being unpredictable, so plans may need to be adjusted. This guide offers suggestions for making the most of your trip, rain or shine. Accept the Irish proverb "There's no such thing as bad weather, only unsuitable clothing," and let the rain add to the adventure. Flexibility can result in some of the most authentic travel experiences.

5. Document your Journey

While this guide contains a wealth of information and suggestions, your journey is entirely your own. Keep a travel journal, take photos, and gather mementos along the way. These personal stories and memories are what truly make your adventure come alive and allow you to share the spirit of Ireland with others.

6. Use the Appendices

The appendices are jam-packed with useful information, including a glossary of culinary terms, a calendar of Irish festivals, and packing tips. These resources are intended to assist you with the logistical aspects of your trip, ensuring a smooth and enjoyable experience.

"Emerald Horizons" is more than just a guidebook; it's an invitation to become immersed in Ireland's rich tapestry. By following these suggestions, you will not only discover the beauty and spirit of the Emerald Isle, but also embark on a journey of personal discovery and connectivity. So pack your sense of adventure, an open heart, and a desire to discover, and let Ireland unfold before you in all of its glory.

# SETTING THE SCENE

## The Irish Landscape

Ireland's landscape is a vibrant tapestry of emerald green, ocean blue, and earthy browns, living up to its nickname, the Emerald Isle. From the untamed beauty of its rugged coastlines to the serene undulations of its green hills, Ireland's landscape is more than just a backdrop to the country's rich history and culture; it is a central character in its story. This diverse terrain invites explorers to travel its length and breadth, discovering natural wonders that have inspired poets, artists, and dreamers for centuries.

Rugged Coasts and Majestic Cliffs

Ireland's coastline is a breathtaking sight where the Atlantic Ocean meets land in a display of nature's power and beauty. The Wild Atlantic Way, a scenic route that runs along Ireland's west coast from Donegal to Cork, takes visitors through some of the country's most spectacular maritime landscapes. The Cliffs of Moher, which stand tall on the edge of County Clare, are perhaps the most iconic of Ireland's coastal wonders. These majestic cliffs provide breathtaking views of the Atlantic, where the crashing waves and seabirds' cries create a symphony that reflects the island's untamed spirit.

The coastline is dotted with countless hidden coves, sandy beaches, and ancient harbors, each one telling a story of maritime adventure, from Viking invaders to daring fishermen braving the wild seas. Exploring these coasts reveals a raw, elemental connection between land and water that underpins much of Ireland's appeal.

Green Hills and Enchanted Valleys

As you travel further inland, the landscape softens into rolling hills and lush valleys, with green hues that appear to shift and change with the passing clouds. The Irish hills are more than just postcard-perfect green pastures; they are landscapes steeped in myths and legends, with each hillfort and standing stone telling a story.

In counties such as Wicklow, Kerry, and Galway, the hills stretch to the horizon, providing endless opportunities for hiking, cycling, and simply relaxing. Glendalough in the Wicklow Mountains combines history and natural beauty, with ancient monastic ruins set against a backdrop of serene lakes and forested walks.

Mystical Landscapes and Ancient Sites

Ireland's landscape is dotted with ancient sites that appear to emerge from the ground itself. The UNESCO World Heritage Site of Brú na Bóinne in County Meath, including Newgrange, showcases Ireland's ancient past, featuring megalithic structures that predate Egypt's pyramids. These ancient sites, set against the backdrop of Ireland's natural beauty, provide a glimpse into the past and a link to the generations who shaped the land.

The Burren in County Clare is another breathtaking landscape, with limestone pavements stretching as far as the eye can see, punctuated by rare flora and megalithic tombs. This one-of-a-kind karst landscape appears to be from another world, showcasing Ireland's natural beauty.

The Living Landscape

Beyond its physical beauty, Ireland's landscape is alive with the presence of those who farm its land, uphold its traditions, and celebrate its natural beauty. The Irish landscape includes patchwork fields surrounded by stone walls in Connemara, traditional peat bogs in the Midlands, and vibrant towns and villages scattered throughout the countryside. This is a land where the past is always present, the rhythm of life changes with the seasons, and the land itself tells the story of its inhabitants.

## Understanding Irish Culture and Traditions

The spirit of Ireland is woven into the fabric of its culture and traditions, forming a vibrant tapestry that reflects the resilience, warmth, and creativity of its people. From music and dance to language and folklore, Irish culture embodies centuries of history, shared experiences, and a strong connection to the land and sea. Understanding the Irish spirit entails accepting the values, traditions, and celebrations that define this distinct island nation.

Music and Dance: The Heartbeat of Ireland

Music and dance are central to Irish culture, serving as both sources of joy and means of storytelling. Traditional Irish music, with its fiddles, tin whistles, and bodhráns, captures the essence of the land, while lively jigs and reels compel even the most reserved to tap their feet. Music pervades every aspect of Irish life, from raucous sessions in cozy pubs to polished performances by professional musicians, bridging generations and communities.

Irish dance, with its intricate footwork and spirited rhythms, is another beloved tradition that captivates audiences around the world. Irish dance, from céilí to step dancing, reflects the resilience and spirit of the Irish people. It celebrates both individual talent and collective heritage.

Language and Literature: Preserving the Gaelic Language

The Irish language, also known as Gaelic or Gaeilge, is significant in Irish culture as a symbol of national identity and heritage. Though English is the most widely spoken language in Ireland today, efforts to preserve and promote Gaelic have continued, with Irish language schools (Gaelscoileanna) and cultural organizations dedicated to its revival.

Festivals and Celebrations: Embracing the Craic

Irish festivals and celebrations provide a glimpse into the heart of Irish culture, where hospitality, conviviality, and good humor are paramount. St. Patrick's Day, the quintessential Irish holiday celebrated all over the world, is a day filled with parades, music, and revelry in honor of Ireland's patron saint and all things green. Beyond the shamrocks and Guinness, there are numerous other festivals that highlight the richness of Irish culture, ranging from traditional music festivals like Fleadh Cheoil to literary gatherings like the Dublin Writers Festival.

## ESSENTIAL TRAVEL TIPS

Planning Your Journey: Best Times to Visit

**Spring (March – May)**

Spring brings milder weather and longer days, with average temperatures ranging from 7°C to 13°C (45°F to 55°F). Expect some rain and rapidly changing weather conditions.

St. Patrick's Day, March 17th, is Ireland's most celebrated holiday, with parades, music, and festivities taking place all over the country.

As spring arrives, wildflowers bloom in the countryside, particularly along the Wild Atlantic Way and in national parks such as Killarney and Connemara.

Witness the spectacle of sheep shearing on farms across rural Ireland, providing insight into traditional farming practices.

Tips
Dress in layers to accommodate changing temperatures and unexpected rain showers.

Popular tourist destinations may see increased demand during the St. Patrick's Day festivities, so book your accommodations well in advance.

**Summer (June to August)**

Summer has the longest days and the warmest temperatures, with average highs ranging from 16°C to 20°C (61°F-68°F). Rainfall remains common, but the days are generally drier and sunnier.

Attend a variety of festivals and cultural events, including music festivals such as the Galway International Arts Festival and outdoor concerts throughout the country.

Outdoor activities include hiking, cycling, and water sports in Ireland's national parks, coastal trails, and scenic lakes and rivers.

Take advantage of the longer daylight hours to explore Ireland's landscapes and attractions late into the evening.

Tips

Summer is Ireland's peak tourist season, so accommodations can fill up quickly, particularly in popular tourist destinations.

Carry a reusable water bottle to stay hydrated, especially when doing outdoor activities in the sun.

**Autumn (September–November)**

Autumn has cooler temperatures and shorter days, with average highs ranging from 14°C to 17°C (57°F to 63°F). Rainfall increases throughout the season, and winds may pick up along the coast.

Witness the spectacular foliage as trees turn gold, orange, and red, especially in national parks such as Killarney and Wicklow.

Enjoy seasonal delights at food festivals celebrating Ireland's harvest, such as the Galway International Oyster Festival and the Kinsale Gourmet Festival.

Quiet Trails: As the peak tourist season comes to an end, enjoy quieter trails and attractions, allowing for a more peaceful and intimate exploration of Ireland's landscape.

Tips

Pack waterproof clothing and layers to prepare for rainy days and cooler temperatures.

Some attractions and accommodations may have reduced hours or seasonal closures, so check ahead of time before planning your trip.

## Winter (December - February)

Winter has the lowest temperatures and shortest days, with average highs ranging from 5°C to 9°C (41°F to 48°F). Rainfall is common, but snowfall is possible, especially at higher elevations.

Enjoy the warmth and camaraderie of traditional Irish pubs, which feature live music and crackling fires to create a welcoming atmosphere.

Take a brisk walk along deserted beaches, coastal cliffs, and forested trails, followed by a hearty meal at a cozy restaurant.

Cities such as Dublin, Galway, and Cork offer a festive atmosphere with Christmas markets, holiday lights, and seasonal events.

Tips

To stay comfortable in colder weather, dress in layers and bring a waterproof jacket, hat, and gloves.

Plan indoor activities. Prepare for shorter daylight hours and inclement weather by scheduling indoor activities like museum visits and cultural experiences.

**Overall Tips for Planning Your Visit**

Consider visiting during the shoulder seasons of spring and autumn to enjoy milder temperatures, fewer crowds, and vibrant seasonal colors.

To experience Ireland's cultural heritage and traditions, look into local events, festivals, and holidays that will be held during your visit.

Prepare for changing weather conditions and create flexible itineraries to accommodate unexpected changes.

Booking accommodations in advance, particularly during peak tourist seasons and major events, ensures availability and peace of mind.

Getting There

**Airports**

Dublin Airport (DUB) is Ireland's largest and busiest airport, serving as a major international gateway with direct flights to destinations around the world. The airport, located about 10 kilometers north of Dublin's city center, provides a variety of amenities such as shops, restaurants, and transportation.

Shannon Airport (SNN): Located in County Clare, Shannon Airport is another major international airport that provides direct flights to Europe, North America, and the Middle East. The airport is located approximately 24 kilometers west of Limerick City Center and provides easy access to Ireland's scenic west coast.

Cork Airport (ORK): Cork Airport, located just outside Cork City in County Cork, provides domestic and international flights with connections to major European hubs. The airport offers convenient access to Ireland's southwest region, which includes the Wild Atlantic Way and the picturesque counties of Cork and Kerry.

Belfast International Airport (BFS) and Belfast City Airport (BHD) are located in Northern Ireland and provide domestic and international flights to destinations throughout the United Kingdom, Europe, and beyond.

Regional Airports: In addition to the major international airports, Ireland has several regional airports, including Kerry Airport (KIR), Knock Airport (NOC), and Waterford Airport (WAT), which provide easy access to specific areas of the country.

**Ferries**

Dublin Port, located on Ireland's east coast, serves as the primary ferry terminal for routes to and from the UK and Europe. Ferry operators such as Irish Ferries and Stena

Line provide regular crossings to UK ports such as Holyhead, Liverpool, and Fishguard, as well as destinations in France and the Netherlands.

Rosslare Europort, located in County Wexford on Ireland's southeast coast, provides ferry services to and from Wales and France. Irish Ferries and Stena Line operate ferries between Rosslare and ports in Pembroke, Fishguard, and Cherbourg, making it easy for visitors from the United Kingdom and mainland Europe to reach the island.

Cork Ferry Terminal, also known as Ringaskiddy Ferry Terminal, operates ferry services to and from Roscoff, France. Brittany Ferries operates these crossings, which provide an alternative route for travelers wishing to explore Ireland and France by sea.

Transport Options for Navigating Ireland

**Public Transport**

a. Bus Services (Bus Éireann): Bus Éireann offers comprehensive coverage across Ireland, connecting cities, towns, and rural areas. The network provides intercity and regional services, with comfortable coaches outfitted with amenities like Wi-Fi and onboard restrooms.

b. Train Services (Irish Rail): Irish Rail, also known as Iarnród Éireann, operates train services that connect major cities and towns throughout Ireland. The network includes commuter services, intercity trains, and scenic routes, offering travelers a comfortable and convenient way to explore the country.

c. Tram Services (Luas): Dublin's light rail system, known as Luas, is comprised of two lines—the Green Line and the Red Line—that provide efficient transportation throughout the city and its suburbs. Luas provides a convenient way to get to Dublin's popular attractions, shopping districts, and cultural hubs.

**Car Rental**

Renting a car gives you the flexibility and freedom to explore Ireland's scenic landscapes, quaint villages, and hidden gems at your leisure. International car rental companies operate at major airports and cities, providing a diverse range of vehicles to accommodate varying travel preferences and group sizes. Ireland's well-maintained road network, which includes scenic driving routes like the Wild Atlantic Way and the Ring of Kerry, makes road trips a popular choice for adventurers.

**Ferry Service**

Ferry services connect Ireland to the United Kingdom and continental Europe, offering an alternative mode of transportation for those arriving by sea. The main ferry terminals are Dublin Port and Rosslare Europort, which serve routes to ports in the United Kingdom, France, and Holland. Operators such as Irish Ferries and Stena Line provide regular crossings with onboard amenities, dining options, and cabin accommodations.

**Cycling and Walking**

Cycling and walking provide immersive experiences through Ireland's stunning landscapes and charming countryside for eco-conscious travelers and outdoor enthusiasts alike. Dedicated cycling routes, such as the Great Western Greenway and the Waterford Greenway, offer scenic trails for cyclists of all skill levels. Similarly, long-distance walking trails like the Wicklow Way and the Kerry Way allow you to explore Ireland's natural beauty on foot, with lodging options ranging from cozy guesthouses to wilderness campsites.

**Taxi Service and Ride Sharing**

Taxi services are widely available in cities and tourist destinations for short-distance travel or convenient transfers to airports, train stations, and accommodations. Ride-sharing platforms such as Uber, as well as local alternatives, provide additional transportation options in cities such as Dublin, Cork, and Galway, giving travelers more flexibility and convenience.

## Guided tours and Transportation

Travelers looking for curated experiences and local insights can explore Ireland's attractions, landmarks, and cultural sites with guided tours and transportation services. Tour operators provide a wide range of options, including day tours, multi-day excursions, and themed experiences focused on specific interests such as history, food, and outdoor adventure.

## Staying Connected in Ireland

**SIM Cards**

a) Prepaid SIM Cards: Buying a prepaid SIM card from a local provider is one of the most convenient and cost-effective ways to use mobile data and make phone calls while in Ireland. Major network operators, such as Vodafone, Three, and Eir, provide a variety of prepaid SIM card options with varying data allowances and validity periods. SIM cards are available at airports, convenience stores, and mobile phone shops across the country.

b. Requirements: To buy and activate a prepaid SIM card, you'll usually need to show a valid form of identification, such as a passport or driver's license. Some providers may also require proof of address, so bring the necessary documentation with you when purchasing a SIM card.

c. Data Plans: Once you've purchased a SIM card, you can select from a range of data plans to meet your needs, including short-term bundles and long-term packages with larger data allowances. Most providers provide ways to top up your credit online, via mobile apps, or at retail locations.

**Wi-Fi**

a. Accommodation: In Ireland, many hotels, hostels, and guesthouses provide free Wi-Fi access for guests to stay connected while relaxing.

b. Cafés and Restaurants: Throughout Ireland, many cafés, restaurants, and bars offer free Wi-Fi to customers. Enjoy a cup of coffee or a delicious meal while catching up on emails or browsing the web.

c. Public Spaces: Visitors may have access to free Wi-Fi at public libraries, tourist information centers, and some public parks. Keep an eye out for Wi-Fi hotspot signs in public spaces.

**Mobile Apps**

a. Navigation Apps: Google Maps, Apple Maps, and Waze are essential for navigating Ireland's roads and public transportation networks. Download offline maps to avoid using mobile data while traveling.

b. Transportation Apps: Apps such as Dublin Bus, Irish Rail, and Luas offer real-time information on public transportation schedules, routes, and ticket purchases, making it easier to navigate cities and towns.

c. Travel Guides: Apps such as TripAdvisor, Lonely Planet, and Visit Ireland provide destination guides, recommendations, and reviews to help you plan your itinerary and discover hidden gems while traveling.

**International Roaming**

a. Packages: If you want to use your current mobile phone plan while traveling in Ireland, check with your home network provider about international roaming packages. These packages may include discounts on international calls, texts, and data usage.

b. Roaming Charges: Be aware of potential roaming charges, as data usage and calls made outside your home country may result in additional fees. To avoid unexpected charges, consider turning off automatic updates and limiting your data usage.

**Portable Wi-Fi Devices**

a. Mobile Hotspots: Portable Wi-Fi devices, also known as mobile hotspots or pocket Wi-Fi, offer convenient internet access on the go. These devices use cellular networks to create a Wi-Fi network that multiple devices can connect to, allowing you to stay connected without the need for public Wi-Fi or local SIM cards.

b. Rental Services: Several companies provide portable Wi-Fi rental services to tourists visiting Ireland. Renting a mobile hotspot provides you with consistent internet access throughout your trip, regardless of your location.

Money Matters

**Currency**

a. Euro (EUR): Ireland's official currency is the euro (€). It is represented by the symbol "€" and is used in all transactions within the country. Banknotes come in denominations of €5, €10, €20, €50, €100, €200, and

€500, while coins come in denominations of 1 cent, 2 cents, 5 cents, 10 cents, 20 cents, 50 cents, €1 and €2.

b. Currency Exchange: Banks, exchange offices, airports, and some hotels all provide currency exchange services. It is recommended that you compare exchange rates and fees before exchanging currency to ensure you get the best value for your money.

**Banking**

a. Major banks in Ireland, including Allied Irish Banks (AIB), Bank of Ireland, Ulster Bank, and Permanent TSB, serve customers across the country. These banks' branches are located in cities, towns, and rural areas, and offer a variety of banking services such as currency exchange, ATM access, and account management.

b. ATMs: Automated Teller Machines (ATMs), also known as cash machines or cashpoints, are widely available across Ireland. ATMs accept major international credit and debit cards, so you can withdraw cash in Euros. Be aware that some ATMs may charge fees for cash withdrawals, particularly if you use a foreign card.

c. Credit and debit cards are widely accepted in Ireland, especially in cities, hotels, restaurants, and retail stores. The most commonly accepted cards are Visa and

MasterCard, followed by American Express and Discover. Contactless payments with cards or mobile devices are becoming more popular in Ireland.

d. Currency Conversion Fees: When using credit or debit cards in Ireland, be aware that your card issuer may charge currency conversion fees. Some banks may also charge foreign transaction fees for purchases made in a currency other than your own.

**Budgeting**

a. Cost of Living: Ireland has a moderate cost of living that varies based on location, accommodation, dining preferences, and activities. Major cities, such as Dublin and Galway, are generally more expensive than rural areas and small towns.

b. Accommodation: Ireland has a wide range of accommodation options, from low-cost hostels and guesthouses to luxury hotels and vacation rentals. When budgeting for accommodation expenses, research your options ahead of time and take into account factors like location, amenities, and reviews.

c. Dining: Dining options in Ireland range from casual pub fare to fine dining experiences. Make a budget for meals and drinks, keeping in mind that prices can vary depending on the establishment and location.

d. Transportation costs in Ireland may include public transportation fares, car rental fees, fuel costs, and parking fees. To save money, research transportation options and plan your trip accordingly.

e. Activities and Attractions: Make a budget for activities and attractions that align with your interests and preferences. Many museums, galleries, and cultural sites offer free or discounted admission on specific days; take advantage of these opportunities to save money.

f. Contingency Fund: It's a good idea to set aside money for unexpected expenses or emergencies while traveling in Ireland. Having a buffer in your budget can provide peace of mind and ensure you're ready for any unexpected events.

# THE MUST-SEE CITIES

Dublin: The Heartbeat of Ireland

Dublin, Ireland's capital city, exudes a dynamic energy that reflects its rich history, vibrant culture, and cosmopolitan charm. From its historic landmarks to its bustling streets, Dublin captures the essence of Irish urban life, providing visitors with an enthralling blend of tradition and innovation.

Dublin's streets are steeped in history, with iconic landmarks commemorating centuries of heritage. Visitors can explore the imposing walls of Dublin Castle, which has served as a symbol of British rule and Irish sovereignty for centuries. Trinity College, Ireland's oldest university, beckons with its cobblestoned squares and the breathtaking Long Room of the Old Library, which houses the ancient Book of Kells.

The city is home to numerous cultural institutions that honor Ireland's artistic heritage as well as contemporary creativity. Museums like the National Museum of Ireland and the Irish Museum of Modern Art (IMMA) provide insight into the country's archaeological treasures and modern art movements. The Abbey Theatre, founded in 1904, is still a shining example of Irish drama, presenting innovative productions that captivate audiences around the world.

As the sun sets, Dublin's streets come alive with music and laughter, as both locals and visitors enjoy the city's legendary nightlife. Traditional pubs, such as The Brazen Head, which dates back to 1198, host live music performances featuring fiddles and bodhráns. Trendy cocktail bars and chic nightclubs add a modern twist to Dublin's social scene, ensuring there is something for everyone to enjoy after dark.

Dublin, with its rich tapestry of history, culture, and hospitality, is truly Ireland's heartbeat. Whether exploring its historic landmarks, immersing oneself in its literary legacy, or simply soaking up its vibrant atmosphere, Dublin welcomes visitors to experience the essence of Irish urban life in all its splendor.

## Historical Dublin Landmarks to Explore

### Dublin Castle

Dublin Castle, built in the 13th century, represents power and authority throughout Ireland's history. Its complex of buildings, which includes the State Apartments and the Chapel Royal, represents a variety of architectural styles spanning centuries.

Discover the majestic interiors of the State Apartments, which are adorned with ornate decorations and historical artifacts. Admire the Chapel Royal's Gothic architecture and walk through the tranquil gardens that surround the castle.

### Trinity College and the Book of Kells

Trinity College, founded in 1592, is Ireland's oldest university with a distinguished academic legacy. The Long Room of the Old Library, which houses the world-famous Book of Kells, an intricately illustrated medieval manuscript, is the highlight of any Trinity College visit.

Admire the exquisite craftsmanship of the Book of Kells, a masterpiece of medieval art known for its intricate illustrations and vibrant colors. Explore the atmospheric Long Room, which is filled with ancient tomes and busts of notable scholars.

**The Literary Trail**

Dublin has a rich literary heritage, serving as a muse and backdrop for some of the world's most celebrated writers. Follow in the footsteps of literary giants along Dublin's literary trail, where every street corner and pub has a story.

**The James Joyce Center**

The James Joyce Center in Dublin honors one of Ireland's most well-known literary figures, James Joyce. The center, housed in a Georgian townhouse, hosts exhibitions, lectures, and guided tours of Joyce's life and works.

Interactive exhibits and multimedia displays immerse visitors in the world of James Joyce. Join a guided walking tour of Joyce's Dublin, following the landmarks and locations immortalized in his seminal works "Ulysses" and "Dubliners."

**Dublin Writers' Museum**

The Dublin Writers Museum, housed in a beautifully restored Georgian mansion, commemorates the literary legacy of Ireland's greatest writers. The museum's exhibits honor iconic figures such as W.B. Yeats, Oscar Wilde, and Samuel Beckett.

See personal belongings, manuscripts, and memorabilia from Ireland's literary luminaries. Explore the museum's rare book, letter, and portrait collection, which provides insights into the lives and works of the country's literary greats.

**Literary Pub Crawl**

Join a literary pub crawl through Dublin's historic streets, where literature is brought to life in iconic pubs and watering holes. The tour, led by knowledgeable guides and actors, includes storytelling, recitations, and performances, as well as visits to well-known literary locations.

Raise a glass in the same pubs where James Joyce, Brendan Behan, and Flann O'Brien once met to talk about their latest literary projects. Listen to readings from iconic works of Irish literature and engage in lively discussions about Dublin's literary legacy.

## Pubs, Music, and Nightlife

### Traditional Irish Pubs

The Brazen Head

The Brazen Head, founded in 1198, is Ireland's oldest pub, rich in history and character. Its cozy interiors, low ceilings, and roaring fireplaces create a welcoming environment in which locals and visitors can enjoy traditional Irish hospitality.

Highlights: Enjoy hearty pub fare and a pint of Guinness while taking in the pub's unique atmosphere. Experience live music sessions featuring talented musicians performing traditional Irish tunes, resulting in an authentic pub experience that should not be missed.

The Temple Bar

The Temple Bar, located in Dublin's cultural quarter, is a well-known pub with a vibrant atmosphere and lively crowds. With its distinctive red facade and bustling beer garden, it's a popular hangout for both locals and tourists.

Highlights: Immerse yourself in The Temple Bar's vibrant atmosphere, where live music spills out onto the streets and revelers congregate to enjoy the craic. While mingling with other pubgoers from all over the world, sample a diverse selection of Irish whiskies and craft beers.

**Live Music Venues**

The Cobblestone

The Cobblestone, located in Dublin's historic Smithfield district, is a well-known music venue that honors Ireland's traditional musical heritage. Its intimate setting and welcoming atmosphere make it a popular destination for musicians and music lovers.

Highlights: Authentic Irish music sessions, known as "seisiúns," feature talented musicians playing traditional tunes on fiddles, tin whistles, and bodhráns. Join in the fun or simply relax and enjoy the lively atmosphere of this popular music pub.

Whelan's

Whelan's is a landmark music venue in Dublin, known for its eclectic mix of live performances and intimate shows. With multiple stages and a diverse range of acts, it serves as a gathering place for both emerging artists and established bands.

Highlights: Enjoy a live concert by local bands, touring artists, or up-and-coming musicians in the intimate setting of Whelan's. From rock and indie to folk and jazz, this iconic Dublin venue has something for everyone's musical tastes.

**Nightlife Hotspots**

The Workman's Club

The Workman's Club is a popular Dublin nightlife destination that offers a variety of live music, DJ sets, and late-night entertainment. It has multiple floors, eclectic decor, rooftop terraces, and a relaxed atmosphere.

Highlights: The Workman's Club's regular club nights and DJ sets feature indie, electro, and alternative beats that will keep you dancing all night. Relax with a cocktail on the rooftop terrace and enjoy panoramic views of Dublin's skyline under the stars.

Dice Bar

Dice Bar, tucked away in the bustling streets of Dublin's city center, is a hidden gem beloved by locals for its retro decor, craft cocktails, and eclectic playlist. With its intimate setting and relaxed atmosphere, it's ideal for a night out with friends.

Highlights: Enjoy expertly crafted cocktails and craft beers while listening to a diverse mix of music ranging from funk and soul to indie and rock. Enjoy the relaxed atmosphere and friendly vibes of this popular Dublin hangout.

## Dublin for Foodies

### Markets

Temple Bar Food Market

The Temple Bar Food Market, located in Dublin's cultural quarter, is a thriving hub of artisanal food producers, local farmers, and gourmet vendors. The market is open every Saturday and offers a wide variety of fresh produce, homemade treats, and artisanal delights.

Highlights: Try a variety of Irish cheeses, cured meats, and freshly baked breads from local producers. Indulge in street food favorites like gourmet burgers, wood-fired pizzas, and authentic falafel wraps while taking in the lively atmosphere of the market.

Dublin Flea Market

The Dublin Flea Market, which takes place on the last Sunday of each month, is a treasure trove of vintage finds, handmade crafts, and delicious street food. Browse stalls selling one-of-a-kind artisanal products, antiques, and collectibles while enjoying live music and entertainment.

Highlights: Sample a wide variety of culinary delights, such as international street food, gourmet pastries, and specialty coffee. This eclectic market offers flavors from all over the world while you browse through eclectic collections of clothing, jewelry, and homeware.

**Café**

Brother Hubbard

Brother Hubbard is a popular Dublin café known for its warm hospitality, welcoming atmosphere, and delicious Middle Eastern-inspired cuisine. With two locations in the city, it's a popular breakfast, brunch, and lunch spot.

Highlights: Enjoy delicious dishes like shakshuka, falafel wraps, and mezze platters made with locally sourced ingredients and exotic spices. For the ultimate café experience, pair your meal with artisanal tea or specialty coffee.

Queen of Tarts

Queen of Tarts is a charming café and bakery located in Dublin's historic city center. It is a popular spot for sweet treats and indulgent afternoon teas, thanks to its reputation for delectable cakes, pastries, and desserts.

Highlights: Enjoy a slice of homemade carrot cake, a freshly baked scone with clotted cream and jam, or a rich chocolate brownie. For the perfect afternoon pick-me-up, pair your sweet treat with a pot of loose-leaf tea or freshly brewed coffee.

**Restaurants**

Chapter One.

Chapter One is a Michelin-starred restaurant in the heart of Dublin, providing an elegant dining experience that highlights the best Irish ingredients and culinary craftsmanship. Led by renowned chef Ross Lewis, the restaurant's seasonal menus feature modern Irish cuisine with a creative twist.

Highlights: Indulge in a gourmet tasting menu that includes exquisite dishes like Irish beef tartare, seared scallops, and roast loin of venison, all paired with expertly curated wines. Dining at Chapter One is an unforgettable experience thanks to its impeccable service, elegant surroundings, and culinary excellence.

The Winding Stair.

The Winding Stair is a popular restaurant overlooking the River Liffey, known for its use of sustainable, locally sourced ingredients and hearty Irish fare. It's a popular destination for those who enjoy good food and literary charm.

Highlights: Enjoy traditional Irish dishes with a modern twist, such as Guinness and beef stew, wild Irish salmon, and artisanal cheese boards featuring the best of Irish dairy. For an unforgettable dining experience, pair your meal with a selection of fine wines, craft beers, or traditional Irish whiskies.

## Cork: Gateway to the South

Cork, also known as the Rebel County, is the vibrant gateway to Ireland's scenic southern region. Cork, with its charming streets lined with colorful Georgian buildings, thriving culinary scene, and proximity to stunning coastal landscapes, welcomes visitors and offers a wealth of experiences to discover.

One of Cork's most famous attractions, the English Market is a foodie's dream, filled with artisanal produce, gourmet delicacies, and local specialties. Wander through the bustling aisles, sampling freshly baked bread, Irish cheeses, and succulent seafood from the nearby coast.

A short drive from Cork City, Cobh is a picturesque town known for its maritime history and colorful waterfront. Explore attractions like the Titanic Experience Cobh, which tells the story of the RMS Titanic's ill-fated voyage, or take a stroll along the promenade to enjoy the scenic views of Cork Harbour.

Cork's vibrant city center and picturesque coastal towns combine to create a captivating blend of history, culture, and gastronomy that invites visitors to explore its diverse landscapes and vibrant communities. Cork welcomes visitors to experience the warmth and hospitality of Ireland's southern region, whether they are wandering through bustling markets, indulging in gourmet cuisine, or taking in the coastal scenery.

### The English Market and Beyond

Begin your journey at the English Market, where you'll find a wide variety of fresh produce, artisanal goods, and gourmet treats. Browse through stalls full of colorful fruits and vegetables, fragrant herbs and spices, and locally sourced meats and cheeses.

The market's fishmongers serve up the region's freshest seafood, including shellfish, smoked salmon, and freshly caught fish. Savor succulent oysters shucked to order, or try a flavorful traditional seafood chowder.

Meet the passionate artisans and producers who showcase their work at the English Market, ranging from bakers and chocolatiers to cheesemakers and charcuterie. Handcrafted chocolates, artisanal cheeses, and freshly baked breads showcase the region's culinary heritage.

Explore Cork's farm-to-table dining scene, where chefs use local ingredients to create innovative dishes. Cork's dining scene caters to all tastes, from traditional Irish fare to international cuisine with a modern twist.

Enjoy a seafood feast at waterfront restaurants and shacks along Cork's scenic coast. Feast on platters of fresh lobster, crab, and prawns, accompanied by locally sourced oysters and a crisp white wine.

Celebrate Cork's thriving craft beer and whiskey scene with tastings and tours at the region's breweries and distilleries. Sample a variety of artisanal brews and single malt whiskies while learning about the rich history and craftsmanship behind each sip.

Culinary experiences in Cobh and Kinsale include visiting the picturesque town of Cobh, which combines maritime history with culinary delights. Explore the waterfront's seafood restaurants, local markets showcasing artisanal products, and the Titanic Experience Cobh, which teaches about the town's Titanic connection.

Explore the culinary treasures of Kinsale, dubbed the "Gourmet Capital of Ireland." Stroll down the town's charming streets, which are lined with award-winning restaurants, artisanal food shops, and cozy pubs. Enjoy fresh seafood, artisanal cheeses, and gourmet cuisine inspired by the region's rich land and sea.

Immerse yourself in Cork's culinary culture by taking hands-on cooking classes taught by local chefs and culinary professionals. Learn how to make traditional Irish dishes, bake homemade bread, and master the art of seafood cooking with the freshest local ingredients.

Exploring Kinsale and Cobh

Kinsale and Cobh, located along County Cork's rugged coastline, entice visitors with their maritime heritage, vibrant architecture, and culinary delights. Set out on a journey to discover the coastal charms of these two enchanting locations.

**Kinsale: The Gourmet Capital of Ireland**

Kinsale, known as the "Gourmet Capital of Ireland," features a historic harbor. Begin your journey through Kinsale's historic harbor, where colorful boats bob in the gentle waves against a backdrop of charming waterfront buildings. Admire the picturesque scenery and take in the maritime atmosphere that has captivated visitors for centuries.

Discover Kinsale's reputation as the "Gourmet Capital of Ireland" by indulging in its culinary offerings. Wander through the town's narrow streets, which are lined with award-winning restaurants, cozy cafés, and artisanal food shops that sell everything from fresh seafood and cheese to homemade chocolates and gourmet pastries.

Head outside of town to see Charles Fort, a 17th-century star-shaped fortress with panoramic views of Kinsale Harbor and the surrounding countryside. Explore the fort's ramparts, tunnels, and historic buildings while learning about its fascinating history as a strategic military stronghold.

**Cobh: A Maritime Legacy**

Discover Cobh's maritime legacy by visiting the Titanic Experience Cobh, which is housed in the original White Star Line ticket office. Step back in time to 1912 and discover the tragic story of the RMS Titanic, which made its final stop in Cobh before embarking on its ill-fated journey.

Take a stroll along Cobh's waterfront promenade to enjoy breathtaking views of Cork Harbour and watch ships sail in and out of port. Pause to read the heartfelt messages left at the town's memorial to the victims of the Lusitania, which was torpedoed off the coast of Cobh during World War I.

Take a short ferry ride from Cobh to Spike Island, a historic island fortress with an intriguing history. Explore the island's military barracks, prison cells, and Victorian-era structures, and learn about its history as a monastic settlement, military base, and prison over the centuries.

Enjoy artisanal delights from Kinsale and Cobh's local producers, such as handmade chocolates, artisanal cheeses, and traditional Irish baked goods. Explore local markets and specialty shops to find unique flavors and culinary treasures to take home as souvenirs.

Take a scenic drive along Ireland's stunning coastal route from Kinsale to Donegal. Wind your way along cliffside roads, past rugged headlands, and through quaint seaside villages, with breathtaking views of the Atlantic Ocean at every turn.

Put on your walking shoes and explore the coastal paths and cliffside trails that wind along the Kinsale and Cobh coastlines. Enjoy invigorating walks with panoramic views of the coastline, fresh sea air, and chances to see local wildlife like seals, seabirds, and possibly dolphins playing in the waves.

Galway: The Cultural Soul of Ireland

Nestled on the windswept shores of Galway Bay, the city of Galway captivates visitors with its rich cultural heritage, vibrant arts scene, and friendly locals. Galway embodies the essence of Irish culture and creativity, from its vibrant streets full of music and laughter to its breathtaking coastal landscapes and historic landmarks.

Explore Galway's historic landmarks, including Eyre Square, a bustling public park with historic buildings, shops, and cafés. Admire the statue of Irish literary giant Padraig Pearse and take in the vibrant atmosphere of this bustling city center.

Discover Galway's history and heritage at the Galway City Museum, which is located on the banks of the River

Corrib. Explore exhibits about the city's medieval origins, maritime heritage, and cultural traditions, which include artifacts, artworks, and interactive displays.

Enjoy traditional Irish cuisine and local specialties at Galway's cozy pubs and acclaimed restaurants. In atmospheric pubs like Tig Coili and Tigh Neachtain's, you can enjoy hearty stews, fresh seafood, and traditional Irish music, or dine on innovative cuisine at award-winning restaurants like Aniar and Kai.

Galway, with its vibrant culture, rich heritage, and breathtaking scenery, embodies the essence of Ireland. Whether you're immersed in the city's artistic traditions, savoring its culinary delights, or exploring its breathtaking natural beauty, Galway invites you to experience the Emerald Isle's magic in all its glory.

Street Performers and Seafront Strolls

**Street Performers Hotspots**

a. Shop Street: Begin your search for Galway's street performers on Shop Street, the bustling pedestrian thoroughfare that serves as the city's entertainment district. Talented musicians, dancers, and entertainers captivate passers-by with their lively performances and contagious energy.

b. Spanish Arch: Walk down to the historic Spanish Arch, where the cobblestone streets are filled with the sounds of buskers and street musicians. Marvel at the performers' skill and creativity as they perform in front of Galway's iconic medieval archway.

c. Eyre Square: Visit Eyre Square, where you'll find a lively mix of street performers and artists demonstrating their skills in this popular gathering place. From magicians and mime artists to fire dancers and acrobats, there is always something exciting to see and do in Galway's vibrant public spaces.

**Locations for Seafront Strolls**

a. Salthill Promenade: Enjoy a peaceful stroll away from the city center. This picturesque coastal walkway provides breathtaking views of Galway Bay and the Atlantic Ocean, making it ideal for a relaxing afternoon stroll or a romantic sunset walk.

b. Blackrock Diving Tower: Brave the cool waters of the Atlantic for a refreshing dip at the iconic Blackrock Diving Tower. Perched on the edge of Galway Bay, this historic diving platform is a popular spot for both locals and visitors to enjoy a refreshing swim or soak up the sun on a hot summer day.

c. Claddagh: Discover the historic fishing village of Claddagh, with traditional thatched cottages and quaint cobblestone streets that evoke the charm of old-world Ireland. Wander along the waterfront and watch local fishermen repair their nets or cast their lines into the sparkling waters of Galway Bay.

**Cultural Encounters**

a. Galway Arts Festival: Experience Galway's vibrant arts scene at the Galway International Arts Festival, offering a diverse program of music, theater, visual arts, and street performances. The festival features avant-garde installations and cutting-edge performances, showcasing the best of Irish and international talent.

b. Latin Quarter: Visit Galway's historic Latin Quarter, which features narrow medieval streets lined with lively pubs, eclectic shops, and vibrant street art. Join a guided walking tour to discover hidden gems while learning about the area's rich history and cultural heritage.

## THE GREAT OUTDOORS

The Wild Atlantic Way

Take an unforgettable journey along the Wild Atlantic Way, a scenic coastal route that stretches over 2,500 kilometers along Ireland's rugged western coastline. From dramatic cliffs and pristine beaches to charming villages and ancient ruins, the Wild Atlantic Way provides a one-of-a-kind road trip experience, inviting visitors to discover Ireland's natural beauty and cultural richness along its wild and windswept Atlantic coast.

**Exploring the Coastal Landscape**

a. Cliffs of Moher: Admire the breathtaking beauty of the Cliffs of Moher, which tower over 200 meters above the Atlantic Ocean. Take a stroll along the cliff-top trails to enjoy panoramic views of the Aran Islands, Galway Bay, and the Twelve Bens Mountain Range.

b. Connemara National Park: Immerse yourself in the rugged beauty of Connemara National Park, which features pristine lakes, boglands, and dramatic mountain scenery. Explore miles of hiking trails, look for native wildlife like Connemara ponies and red deer, and marvel at the ancient stone forts and megalithic tombs scattered throughout the park.

Coastal Villages and Hidden Gems

a. Dingle Peninsula: Discover coastal villages and hidden gems on the Dingle Peninsula, a scenic stretch of the Wild Atlantic Way. Along this rugged coastline, you'll find colorful fishing villages, ancient archaeological sites, and sandy beaches.

b. Westport: Visit the charming town of Westport, located at the foot of Croagh Patrick mountain and overlooking Clew Bay. Explore the town's historic streets, visit local shops and galleries, and eat delicious seafood at waterfront restaurants that overlook the bay.

Outdoor Adventures and Activities

a. Surfing in County Sligo: Outdoor activities in County Sligo include surfing at world-class beaches and epic swells along the Atlantic coast. Whether you're a seasoned surfer or a beginner looking for your first wave, the Wild Atlantic Way provides plenty of opportunities to hang ten and feel the rush of the ocean.

b. Sea Kayaking in County Kerry: Use a sea kayak to explore the rugged coastline of County Kerry, including hidden coves, sea caves, and sheltered bays. Paddle beneath towering cliffs, spot seals basking on rocky outcrops, and enjoy the tranquility of Ireland's wild and unspoiled Atlantic waters.

## The Cliffs of Moher

Perched dramatically on the western edge of County Clare, overlooking the wild and untamed Atlantic Ocean, the Cliffs of Moher are one of Ireland's most iconic and breathtaking natural landmarks. These majestic cliffs, which rise to heights of over 200 meters at their highest point, provide visitors with a breathtaking view of sheer rock faces, crashing waves, and sweeping vistas that stretch for miles along the rugged coastline.

As you look out over the Atlantic Ocean and the Aran Islands, you will be astounded by the Cliffs of Moher's breathtaking beauty. Marvel at the sheer scale and grandeur of these towering cliffs, carved by the relentless forces of wind and waves over millions of years.

Walk along the cliff-top trails, which wind along the edge of the cliffs and provide breathtaking views at every turn. Take in the sights and sounds of seabirds flying overhead, nesting in rocky crevices, and soaring on updrafts from the churning waters below.

Exlpore the various plants and animals that live on the cliffs and in the surrounding coastal habitats. The Cliffs of Moher are alive and vibrant, with hardy grasses and wildflowers clinging to the cliff faces and marine life like seals and dolphins frolicking in the waters below.

The visitor center at the Cliffs of Moher offers interactive exhibits, audiovisual presentations, and interpretive displays to learn about the landscape's natural and cultural history. Learn about the cliffs' geology, wildlife, and human heritage, as well as practical tips for making the most of your visit.

Take a guided tour of the Cliffs of Moher to learn more about their geology, ecology, and cultural heritage. Knowledgeable guides lead informative and entertaining tours, telling fascinating stories and anecdotes that bring the cliffs to life and deepen your appreciation for their beauty and significance.

Connemara

Connemara, located on Ireland's western coast, is a land of rugged wilderness and untamed beauty, with towering mountains, pristine lakes, and windswept moors combining to form a landscape of breathtaking natural splendor. Connemara, with its remote villages and ancient ruins, wild coastlines, and vast expanses of bogland, gives visitors a glimpse into the soul of Ireland's wild and untamed west.

Discover the majestic Twelve Bens mountain range, a rugged cluster of peaks that rise dramatically from the Connemara landscape. Hike through heather-covered slopes, scramble up rocky ridges, and summit towering peaks to get panoramic views of the surrounding wilderness and the sparkling Atlantic Ocean.

Experience the natural beauty and ecological diversity of Connemara National Park, a pristine wilderness sanctuary spanning over 2,000 hectares of mountains, bogs, and woodlands. Follow scenic hiking trails through ancient oak forests, spot rare and endangered flora and fauna, and take in the breathtaking views from Diamond Hill.

Take a scenic drive along one of Ireland's most stunning coastal routes. Wind your way along cliff-top roads, past secluded beaches, and through charming villages, taking in panoramic views of the Atlantic coast and the rugged beauty of Connemara's wild and windswept shores.

Head out to the remote island of Inishbofin, a hidden gem off the Connemara coast. Explore ancient ruins, walk along sandy beaches, and learn about the island's rich maritime heritage as you wander through its picturesque harbors and fishing villages.

## Cycling in Ireland

### Exploring the Countryside

a. The Great Western Greenway: Explore the countryside by cycling along the Great Western Greenway, Ireland's longest off-road trail. This scenic route runs 42 kilometers through County Mayo and follows the path of an old railway line, providing flat and easy terrain with breathtaking views of Clew Bay, Achill Island, and the Nephin Beg mountain range.

b. Waterford Greenway: Cycle along the Waterford Greenway, a scenic trail that winds through County Waterford's beautiful countryside and coastal landscapes. This family-friendly route from Waterford City to Dungarvan spans 46 kilometers and passes through charming villages, lush woodlands, and historic railway tunnels, with plenty of opportunities to stop and explore along the way.

### Coastal Adventures

a. The Wild Atlantic Way: Cycle along Ireland's west coast to experience the rugged beauty. This iconic coastal route, which stretches over 2,500 kilometers from Donegal to Cork, provides breathtaking views of towering cliffs, sandy beaches, and crashing waves, as well as a variety of terrain ranging from gentle coastal paths to challenging mountain climbs.

b. The Copper Coast: Take a cycling tour along County Waterford's coastal roads and cliff-top trails to enjoy the breathtaking scenery. Follow the Copper Coast Geopark Cycle Route, which runs for 25 kilometers along the coast, passing through picturesque villages, historic sites, and panoramic views of the Irish Sea.

**Mountain Biking Trails**

a. Ballyhoura Mountain Bike Trails: Ballyhoura Mountain Bike Trails is a top destination for mountain biking in Ireland. These purpose-built trails in County Limerick and County Cork provide over 90 kilometers of singletrack routes through dense forests, rocky terrain, and exhilarating downhill descents, catering to riders of all skill levels.

b. Ticknock Mountain Bike Trails: Test your riding skills on the Ticknock Mountain Bike Trails, which are located in the Dublin Mountains and overlooking Dublin. Ticknock's trails range from gentle forest paths to technical downhill descents, providing thrilling rides and breathtaking views of Dublin Bay and the surrounding countryside.

**Canal Paths and Towpaths**

a. Royal Canal Greenway: Cycle along the tranquil waters of the Royal Canal on the Royal Canal Greenway, a scenic trail that connects Dublin and Longford. This flat and easy route of 130 kilometers takes you through picturesque countryside, charming villages, and historic landmarks, with opportunities for boating, fishing, and birdwatching along the way.

b. Grand Canal Way: Take a 117-kilometer trail that follows the Grand Canal from Dublin to Shannon Harbour in County Offaly. Cycle along towpaths and canal banks, passing through picturesque countryside, quaint towns, and historic locks and bridges, with plenty of opportunities to pause and enjoy the tranquil surroundings.

**Family-Friendly Routes**

a. Phoenix Park: Family-friendly routes include a leisurely cycle through Dublin's Phoenix Park, Europe's largest urban park and a popular destination for cyclists of all ages. Explore scenic pathways, woodland trails, and open meadows while pedaling through this green oasis in the heart of the city. Keep an eye out for the park's resident deer herd.

b. Greenways and Trails: Explore a variety of family-friendly cycling routes and greenways throughout Ireland, including coastal paths, riverside trails, forest tracks, and park circuits. With options for riders of all ages and abilities, these scenic routes provide an excellent opportunity to discover Ireland's natural beauty and cultural heritage on two wheels.

**Best National Parks for Hiking**

**Wicklow Mountains National Park**

a. Glendalough Valley: Explore the ancient beauty of Glendalough Valley, which is home to one of Ireland's most famous monastic sites and a network of picturesque hiking trails. Explore this historic valley's glacial valleys, shimmering lakes, and dense woodlands via routes ranging from strolls to strenuous mountain hikes.

b. Lugnaquilla: Climb the Wicklow Mountains' highest peak, Lugnaquilla, on a strenuous mountain hike that rewards intrepid adventurers with panoramic views of the surrounding landscape. Ascend through heather-clad slopes and rocky terrain to the summit, where a clear day allows you to see as far as the Irish Sea and Dublin Bay.

**Killarney National Park**

a. The Kerry Way: Explore Killarney National Park by taking a multi-day trek along the Kerry Way, Ireland's longest signposted walking trail, which passes through breathtaking scenery. Wander through ancient woodlands, past sparkling lakes, and over rolling hills, stopping at historic sites, charming villages, and breathtaking views along the way.

b. Torc Mountain: Hike to the top of Torc Mountain for panoramic views of Killarney's famous lakes and mountains. Follow well-marked trails through oak and yew forests to the rocky summit, where you can take in the views of the McGillycuddy's Reeks mountain range and the shimmering waters of Lough Leane below.

**Connemara National Park**

a. Diamond Hill: Take a rewarding hike up Diamond Hill, Connemara National Park's centerpiece, for breathtaking views of the surrounding wilderness and coastline. Follow well-maintained trails through heather-covered slopes and rocky outcrops until you reach the summit, where you can enjoy panoramic views of Connemara's rugged landscapes.

b. Connemara Way: Explore Connemara's wild beauty on the Connemara Way, a long-distance walking trail that winds through the region's diverse landscapes and cultural heritage. Travel through rolling hills, verdant valleys, and coastal plains, stopping at quaint villages, ancient ruins, and scenic viewpoints along the way.

**Burren National Park**

a. Mullaghmore: Visit Mullaghmore, one of the iconic peaks in Burren National Park, for a challenging hike with stunning views of the limestone plateau and Atlantic coastline. Trek through lunar-like landscapes of karst pavement and limestone terraces, then ascend to the summit to take in the rugged beauty of the Burren.

b. Poulnabrone Dolmen: Take a hike to Poulnabrone Dolmen, a Neolithic burial tomb over 5,000 years old, to learn about the Burren's ancient history and geological wonders. Wander through limestone pavements and verdant meadows to reach this iconic monument, where you can ponder the mysteries of Ireland's ancient past.

**Glenveagh National Park**

a. Mount Errigal: Glenveagh National Park offers a challenging hike to Mount Errigal, the highest peak in County Donegal, with breathtaking views of Glenveagh National Park and the Derryveagh Mountains. Ascend through rocky terrain and scree slopes to the summit, where you can take in the beauty of Donegal's rugged landscape.

b. Glenveagh Castle: Explore the scenic trails and gardens of Glenveagh National Park, which includes the picturesque Glenveagh Castle and its surrounding woodland estate. Wander along tranquil lakeshores, through lush woodlands, and past colorful gardens to immerse yourself in the remote wilderness's natural beauty and serenity.

Surfing and Sea Kayaking Hotspots

a. Bundoran, County Donegal: Bundoran, known as Ireland's surf capital, has some of the best waves on the west coast and attracts surfers from all over the world. Ride the legendary breaks of Tullan Strand and The Peak, where powerful swells and consistent surf conditions provide endless thrills and excitement.

b. Lahinch, County Clare: Discover the vibrant surf scene in Lahinch, a charming seaside town located along the Wild Atlantic Way. Paddle out to the breaks at Lahinch Beach and Crab Island, where rolling waves and sandy bottoms make ideal conditions for surfers of all skill levels, from beginners to seasoned pros.

c. Clew Bay, County Mayo: Explore the stunning landscapes and hidden coves along the rugged coastline. Paddle past ancient ruins, rocky headlands, and pristine beaches, exploring islands like Clare Island and Inishbofin while taking in panoramic views of the surrounding mountains and sea cliffs.

d. Dingle Peninsula, County Kerry: Go sea kayaking around the Dingle Peninsula's dramatic cliffs and sea stacks, which is one of Ireland's most scenic coastal landscapes. Navigate through crystal-clear waters, beneath towering cliffs, and into hidden sea caves, passing seals, dolphins, and seabirds along the way.

e. Achill Island, County Mayo. Discover the rugged beauty of Achill Island's coastline, which features pristine beaches, towering sea cliffs, and turquoise waters. Paddle through secluded bays like Keem Bay and Silver Strand, where golden sands and azure waters provide the ideal setting for a day of sea kayaking adventures.

f. Connemara, County Galway: Explore the wild and unspoiled beauty of Connemara's coastline, which includes secluded coves, hidden beaches, and clear waters. Explore the sheltered bays of Killary Harbour and Bertraghboy Bay, where calm waters and breathtaking scenery make sea kayaking an unforgettable experience.

**Safety and Equipment**

a. Before going out on the water, check the weather, tides, and currents, and become acquainted with local hazards and safety guidelines. Always wear a personal flotation device (PFD) and keep essential safety equipment handy, such as a whistle, paddle leash, and communication device.

b. Invest in high-quality surfing and kayaking equipment, such as a durable surfboard or kayak, wetsuit, paddle, and safety equipment. Consider taking lessons or guided tours with certified instructors to improve your skills and local knowledge, ensuring a safe and enjoyable boating experience.

**Best Golf Courses**

a. Ballybunion Golf Club, County Kerry: Tee off on Ballybunion's legendary links, which are regarded as among the world's best golf courses. Challenge yourself on the Old Course, which boasts dramatic dunes, undulating fairways, and breathtaking views of the Atlantic Ocean, or put your skills to the test on the newer Cashen Course, designed by renowned architect Robert Trent Jones Sr.

b. Royal Portrush Golf Club in County Antrim: Experience the thrill of playing at Royal Portrush, the 2019 Open Championship venue and one of Ireland's most prestigious golf clubs. Navigate the rugged dunes and coastal terrain of the Dunluce Links, complete with challenging bunkers, blind shots, and breathtaking views of the Giant's Causeway and Donegal coastline.

c. The K Club of County Kildare: Play like a pro at The K Club, which hosted the 2006 Ryder Cup and is one of Ireland's premier championship golf resorts. Take on the Arnold Palmer-designed Ryder Cup Course, with its pristine fairways, strategic water hazards, and immaculate conditioning, or put your skills to the test on the Smurfit Course, a challenging parkland layout nestled among lush woodlands and picturesque lakes.

d. Adare Manor in County Limerick: Experience luxury and elegance at Adare Manor, which is home to one of Ireland's most exclusive golf courses and will host the Ryder Cup in 2026. Tee off on the championship course, redesigned by renowned architect Tom Fazio, and take in the pristine fairways, sculpted greens, and breathtaking views of the River Maigue and the majestic manor house.

e. Discover the hidden gem of County Sligo Golf Club, located in Ireland's northwest coast. Play a round on

Rosses Point's famous links, which offer challenging terrain, panoramic views of Benbulbin Mountain, and a rich golfing heritage spanning over a century.

f. Tralee Golf Club, County Kerry: Discover the beauty of Tralee Golf Club, located on the breathtaking Dingle Peninsula and overlooking the Atlantic Ocean. Enjoy the thrill of playing Arnold Palmer's first European design, which features dramatic elevation changes, breathtaking views, and challenging holes that meander through dunes, valleys, and coastal cliffs.

g. Old Head Golf Links in County Cork. Admire the breathtaking beauty of Old Head Golf Links, perched atop a rugged promontory overlooking the Atlantic Ocean. Tee off on cliff-top fairways, navigate coastal hazards, and take in panoramic views of the sea and surrounding countryside on this iconic links course, which exemplifies the beauty and challenge of golf in Ireland.

h. Portmarnock Golf Club, County Dublin: Experience the rich history and tradition of Portmarnock Golf Club, which is located just north of Dublin city. Play a round on the Old Course's classic links, which feature natural dunes, strategic bunkers, and a timeless design that has tested the skills of golfing legends for over a century.

# OFF THE BEATEN PATH

Hidden Villages to Explore

a. Glenbeigh, County Kerry: Discover the charming village of Glenbeigh in County Kerry, nestled on the shores of Dingle Bay and surrounded by the majestic mountains of the Kerry Peninsula, for a tranquil retreat. Explore the quaint streets, traditional pubs, and colorful cottages to immerse yourself in the timeless beauty and tranquillity of this Wild Atlantic Way hidden gem.

b. Cong, County Mayo: Travel back in time to the picturesque village of Cong, which was immortalized in the classic film "The Quiet Man" starring John Wayne and Maureen O'Hara. Wander through its narrow streets, see historic sites like Cong Abbey and Ashford Castle, and discover the enchanting beauty and rich heritage of this idyllic village nestled between Lough Corrib and Lough Mask.

c. Kilmallock, County Limerick. Explore Kilmallock, a medieval town steeped in history and folklore, and uncover its rich tapestry of myths, legends, and ancient traditions. As you wander through its atmospheric streets and historic landmarks, you'll discover stories about knights and kings, saints and scholars, and the mystical world of Irish mythology.

d. Ardara, County Donegal: Learn about the folklore and traditions of Ardara, a quaint village in Donegal's Gaeltacht region. Discover its vibrant music and dance scene, hear tales of faeries and banshees, and learn about the rich cultural heritage and warm hospitality of this hidden gem on Ireland's rugged northwest coast.

e. Ardara, County Donegal: Discover hidden gems and local treasures in Kinsale, County Cork. Explore Kinsale, known as the "Gourmet Capital of Ireland," and discover its hidden gems and local treasures. Sample fresh seafood at its renowned restaurants, browse artisan shops and galleries and enjoy the maritime charm and vibrant atmosphere of this historic town on Ireland's south coast.

f. Ennistymon, County Clare: Discover the hidden beauty of Ennistymon, a quaint market town nestled along the banks of the River Inagh in the heart of the Burren. Discover the secrets of this hidden gem in County Clare by exploring its narrow streets, historic buildings, and cascading waterfalls, as well as experiencing the warmth and hospitality of the local community.

g. Glengarriff, County Cork: Escape to the peaceful beauty of Glengarriff, a picturesque village nestled in the scenic landscapes of West Cork. Discover the breathtaking beauty and hidden treasures of this enchanting coastal retreat by exploring its lush woodlands, tranquil lakes, and exotic gardens, as well as taking scenic walks and boat trips.

h. Carlingford, County Louth: Visit the medieval village of Carlingford, located on the shores of Carlingford Lough beneath the majestic peaks of the Cooley Mountains. Explore its narrow streets, ancient ruins, and scenic harbor, and go on outdoor adventures like hiking, sailing, and mountain biking in the stunning landscapes of Ireland's Ancient East.

Top Ancient Sites to Explore

a. Newgrange, County Meath: Enter the mystical world of Newgrange, a UNESCO World Heritage Site and one of Ireland's most recognizable ancient monuments. Explore this Neolithic passage tomb, built over 5,000 years ago, and learn about astronomy, architecture, and prehistoric art while admiring the massive stone chambers and intricately carved megaliths.

b. Skellig Michael, County Kerry: Visit the remote island of Skellig Michael, a sacred site steeped in mystery and mythology, and explore its ancient monastic settlement perched atop rugged sea cliffs. Climb the steep steps carved into the rock, explore the stone beehive huts and medieval church, and reflect on the spiritual significance of this breathtaking sanctuary in the heart of the Atlantic Ocean.

c. Hill of Tara, County Meath: Discover Ireland's ancient capital and sacred landscape rich in mythology and history. Explore its ancient earthworks, standing stones, and royal enclosures, and immerse yourself in Irish king legends and ancient rituals while looking out over the Boyne Valley's rolling hills.

d. Loughcrew Cairns, County Meath: Visit the mystical hills of Loughcrew, which are home to a collection of ancient passage tombs and megalithic monuments dating back more than 5,000 years. Climb to the summit of Slieve na Calliagh, also known as the Witch's Hill, and explore the Neolithic burial chambers and enigmatic stone carvings dotting the windswept landscape.

e. Poulnabrone Dolmen in County Clare: Discover the enigmatic beauty of Poulnabrone Dolmen, a megalithic tomb from the Neolithic period and one of Ireland's most famous ancient monuments. Marvel at the imposing stone portal and capstone, and ponder the mysteries of this ancient burial site as you consider its place in the Burren's prehistoric landscape.

f. Dun Aengus, County Galway: Discover the dramatic cliff-top fortress of Dun Aengus, located on the edge of Inishmore Island in the Aran Islands archipelago. Wander through its ancient stone walls and defensive ramparts, looking out over the endless expanse of the Atlantic Ocean, as you learn about the secrets of this ancient stronghold and its strategic importance in ancient times.

g. Carrowmore Megalithic Cemetery in County Sligo. Explore the ancient landscape of Carrowmore, which contains one of Ireland's largest and oldest megalithic cemeteries. Explore its collection of prehistoric tombs and stone circles, marveling at their intricate alignments and astronomical significance as you follow in the footsteps of Ireland's early settlers.

h. Knowth, County Meath: Explore the Neolithic passage tomb complex at Brú na Bóinne, a UNESCO World Heritage site. Explore the intricately decorated chambers and massive kerbstones, which are adorned with megalithic art and symbols that reveal the spiritual beliefs and cultural practices of Ireland's ancient inhabitants.

Best **Island Hopping Spots**

a. Aran Islands, County Galway: Take a trip to the Aran Islands, a group of rugged outcrops off the coast of County Galway. Explore Inishmore, the largest island, with its ancient fortresses and windswept landscapes, or head to Inishmaan and Inisheer for a taste of traditional island life and breathtaking coastal scenery.

b. Valentia Island, County Kerry: Explore the enchanting beauty of Valentia Island, located off the coast of the Iveragh Peninsula in County Kerry. Explore the rugged coastline, secluded beaches, and picturesque villages, as well as historic landmarks like the Valentia Island Lighthouse and Geokaun Mountain's dramatic cliffs.

c. Bere Island, County Cork: Find peace on Bere Island, a hidden gem in Bantry Bay off Ireland's southwest coast. Unwind in this secluded island retreat by exploring its scenic walking trails, ancient archaeological sites, and peaceful harbors, as well as experiencing the warmth and hospitality of the local community.

d. Sherkin Island, County Cork: Escape to the idyllic shores of Sherkin Island, located just a short ferry ride from the bustling port town of Baltimore in County Cork. Explore its sandy beaches, rocky coves, and lush woodlands, as well as its rich maritime heritage and artistic community, all set against the stunning backdrop of Roaringwater Bay.

e. Rathlin Island, County Antrim. Set out on an adventure to Rathlin Island, located off the rugged coast of County Antrim in Northern Ireland. Explore the dramatic cliffs, hidden caves, and rugged coastal trails, and stop by the iconic West Light Seabird Centre to see spectacular birdlife and panoramic views of the Atlantic Ocean.

f. Clare Island, County Mayo: Discover the rugged beauty of Clare Island, the largest inhabited island in Clew Bay, off the coast of County Mayo. Hike to Knockmore's summit for breathtaking views of the bay and surrounding islands, explore the historic abbey and medieval castle and immerse yourself in the timeless charm of this remote island paradise.

g. Tory Island, County Donegal Immerse yourself in Tory Island's rich Gaelic culture and artistic traditions, which are located off the coast of County Donegal in the North Atlantic. Explore the island's rugged landscapes, ancient monastic sites, and colorful villages, as well as meet the island's resident artists and musicians, who are inspired by its remote and mystical surroundings.

h. Rathlin Island, County Antrim: Learn about the island's history and heritage, which is steeped in myth and legend and contains ancient ruins and archaeological treasures dating back thousands of years. Visit the ruins of Bruce's Castle, explore the historic lighthouses, and learn about the island's fascinating maritime history and links to Scottish and Irish mythology.

# CULTURAL IMMERSION

Where to Experience Irish Music and Dance

**Musical Hotspots**

a. Temple Bar in Dublin: Immerse yourself in the vibrant atmosphere of Temple Bar, Dublin's cultural quarter, and visit lively pubs and venues where traditional Irish music is performed nightly. Join locals and visitors for spontaneous fiddle, bodhrán, and tin whistle sessions to experience the heart and soul of Irish music in the capital.

b. Doolin, County Clare: Visit the music mecca of Doolin, located on Ireland's rugged west coast, to experience the authentic sounds of traditional Irish music in its purest form. Explore its well-known pubs, including McDermott's and O'Connor's, where world-class musicians perform toe-tapping jigs and reels that echo through the village's cozy streets.

**Festivals and Events**

a. Willie Clancy Summer School, Miltown Malbay: Visit Miltown Malbay, County Clare, for the annual Willie Clancy Summer School, where you can learn about Irish music and dance traditions. Participate in workshops, concerts, and sessions led by master musicians and dancers to honor the legacy of renowned uilleann piper Willie Clancy in the heart of traditional music country.

b. Fleadh Cheoil na hÉireann, Various Locations: Fleadh Cheoil na hÉireann, Ireland's largest traditional music festival, showcases the pinnacle of Irish music and culture. The Fleadh, held annually in various locations across the country, brings together musicians, singers, and dancers from around the world for a week-long celebration of music, dance, and craic.

**Hidden Music Scenes**

a. Ennis, County Clare: This is a picturesque market town with a vibrant music scene and lively pub sessions, making it a hidden gem. Explore its historic streets and medieval architecture, as well as the warmth and hospitality of the locals, by attending impromptu music sessions in cozy pubs like Brogan's Bar and Cruises.

b. West Cork: Get off the beaten path and visit the scenic beauty of West Cork, where traditional music thrives amid the rolling hills and rugged coastline. Explore charming villages like Ballydehob, Bantry, and Schull, as well as intimate sessions in local pubs and community halls where musicians gather late at night to share tunes and stories.

**Dance Workshops**

a. Riverdance Experience in Dublin. The Riverdance Experience in Dublin immerses you in the world of Irish dance, teaching you the steps and techniques of this iconic dance form from professional dancers and choreographers. Discover the history and evolution of Irish dance, as well as your inner dancer, in this fun and interactive workshop for people of all ages and skill levels.

b. Set Dancing Weekends at Various Locations: Join a set dancing weekend in rural Ireland to learn the traditional steps and figures of Irish set dancing in a casual and welcoming setting. Whether you're a beginner or an experienced dancer, these weekends provide an unparalleled opportunity to learn from local experts while immersing yourself in the joy and camaraderie of Irish dance culture.

Festivals Not to Miss

a. St. Patrick's Festival in Dublin. Experience the world-renowned St. Patrick's Festival in Dublin, a multi-day celebration of Irish culture, music, and heritage. Join the colorful parade through Dublin's streets, enjoy live music and entertainment at outdoor concerts and events, and soak up the festive atmosphere of Ireland's national holiday.

b. Galway International Arts Festival: Immerse yourself in Galway's vibrant arts scene with the Galway International Arts Festival, a two-week celebration of music, theater, visual arts, and street performances. Explore Galway's historic streets, which have been transformed into a creative and cultural hub, and discover innovative and inspiring works by both local and international artists.

c. Electric Picnic in County Laois: Electric Picnic, held annually on Stradbally Estate in County Laois, offers the ultimate music and arts festival experience. Electric Picnic is a highlight of the Irish festival calendar, featuring a diverse lineup of music acts across multiple stages, ranging from indie rock to electronic dance music, as well as art installations, food markets, and immersive experiences.

d. Fleadh Cheoil na hÉireann, Several Locations: Fleadh Cheoil na hÉireann is Ireland's largest music festival, celebrating the best of traditional Irish music and culture. Join musicians, singers, and dancers from all over the world for a week-long festival of sessions, workshops, concerts, and competitions that highlight the rich tapestry of Irish music and dance.

e. Taste of Dublin: This is a food and drink festival that showcases Ireland's top chefs, restaurants, and producers. Sample gourmet dishes, artisanal treats, and craft beverages, as well as cooking demonstrations, masterclasses, and culinary experiences that highlight Ireland's rich culinary heritage and innovation.

f. Galway International Oyster Festival: Experience the flavors of the sea at the Galway International Oyster Festival, an annual celebration of seafood and culture in the heart of Galway. Enjoy oyster shucking competitions, seafood tastings, and gourmet dining experiences while taking in the vibrant atmosphere of this iconic festival that has delighted foodies for over six decades.

g. Dublin Book Festival: Immerse yourself in the world of literature by attending the Dublin Book Festival, an annual celebration of Irish and international writing held in Ireland's capital city. Attend author readings, book launches, panel discussions, and workshops to learn about Dublin's vibrant literary scene and rich storytelling traditions, which have earned it UNESCO City of Literature status.

h. William Butler Yeats International Summer School, Sligo: Explore the life and works of Ireland's greatest poet at the W.B. Yeats International Summer School in Sligo, William Butler Yeats' birthplace. Attend lectures, seminars, and cultural events led by leading scholars and writers. Discover the landscapes and inspirations that shaped Yeats' poetic vision and legacy.

# ACCOMMODATIONS

Castle Hotels for a Royal Stay

**Majestic Retreats**

a. Ashford Castle in County Mayo: Experience luxury and grandeur at Ashford Castle, a five-star hotel nestled among 350 acres of manicured gardens and woodlands on the shores of Lough Corrib. Experience the elegance of a bygone era at this historic castle, which dates back to the 13th century and offers opulent interiors, award-winning dining, and a variety of outdoor activities such as falconry, archery, and fishing.

b. Dromoland Castle, County Clare: Enter the regal splendor of Dromoland Castle, a 16th-century fortress nestled among 450 acres of rolling parkland and lakes in County Clare. This luxurious castle hotel offers lavish accommodations, exquisite dining, and impeccable service. Explore the extensive grounds, championship golf course, and spa facilities for an unforgettable royal retreat.

**Historic Hideaways**

a. Waterford Castle Hotel in County Waterford: Escape to the serenity of Waterford Castle Hotel, a 16th-century fortress nestled on a private island in the scenic River Suir. Experience the charm and character of this historic castle, which features elegant rooms, a fine dining restaurant, and a scenic golf course, as well as exclusive access to the island's lush gardens, walking trails, and wildlife sanctuary.

b. Lough Eske Castle, County Donegal: Experience the beauty of Lough Eske Castle, a five-star hotel nestled in 43 acres of woodland and gardens on the shores of Lough Eske in County Donegal. Immerse yourself in luxury and comfort at this restored 17th-century castle, which features spacious suites, gourmet dining, and a serene spa, as well as the warm hospitality and timeless elegance of Ireland's northwest coast.

**Romantic Retreats**

a. Ballynahinch Castle Hotel, County Galway: This hotel offers a romantic retreat with 700 acres of wilderness. Immerse yourself in the natural beauty and tranquility of Ireland's wild west coast by retreating to the serenity of this charming castle hotel, which features cozy rooms, a fine dining restaurant, and scenic walking trails.

b. Kilkea Castle, County Kildare: Relax in luxury and romance at Kilkea Castle, a medieval fortress nestled among 180 acres of lush parkland and gardens in County Kildare. Escape to the elegance of this historic castle, which boasts beautifully appointed rooms, gourmet dining options, and a variety of leisure activities such as golf, horseback riding, and falconry, for an enchanting and unforgettable getaway.

**Family-Friendly Fortresses**

a. Adare Manor in County Limerick: Adare Manor, a grand neo-Gothic castle surrounded by 840 acres of parkland and gardens in County Limerick, offers a royal escape for your family. This opulent castle hotel offers the ultimate in luxury and comfort, with spacious suites, award-winning dining, and world-class amenities like a championship golf course, spa, and children's activity center.

b. Barberstown Castle, County Kildare: Make lasting memories with your family at Barberstown Castle, a historic castle hotel nestled among 20 acres of manicured gardens and woodlands in County Kildare. Experience the warmth and hospitality of this charming castle, complete with cozy accommodations, a traditional Irish pub, and an outdoor playground, and discover the nearby attractions and activities that make Ireland the ideal destination for a family adventure.

Cozy Bed and Breakfasts

**Countryside Charm**

a. Hillcrest Farmhouse in County Kerry: Hillcrest Farmhouse, a charming bed and breakfast nestled in the rolling hills of County Kerry, provides genuine Irish hospitality. Wake up to panoramic views of the lush countryside, eat hearty home-cooked breakfasts made with locally sourced ingredients, and visit nearby attractions such as the Ring of Kerry and Killarney National Park.

b. Gleann Fia Country House, County Clare: Relax at Gleann Fia Country House, a charming bed and breakfast nestled in the scenic landscapes of County Clare. Relax in beautifully appointed rooms with countryside views, enjoy delicious breakfasts with homemade bread and preserves, and explore the beauty of the Burren and Cliffs of Moher, which are just a short drive away.

**Coastal Comfort**

a. Ocean View Bed and Breakfast in County Cork: Relax by the sea at Ocean View Bed and Breakfast, a cozy retreat overlooking Bantry Bay in County Cork. Enjoy your hosts' warm hospitality, wake up to breathtaking ocean views from your room, and begin your day with a hearty Irish breakfast before exploring West Cork's rugged coastline and charming villages.

b. Seaview Guesthouse, County Donegal: Experience the beauty of Donegal's Wild Atlantic Way at Seaview Guesthouse, a welcoming bed and breakfast perched on the cliffs overlooking Donegal Bay. Relax in comfortable rooms with sea views, eat freshly prepared breakfasts with local specialties, and take scenic walks along the coast or visit nearby attractions like Slieve League and Glenveagh National Park.

**Village Vibes**

a. Harbour House Bed and Breakfast, County Galway: Experience the charm of village life at Harbour House Bed and Breakfast, a cozy retreat in the heart of Kinvara, County Galway. Stay in beautifully decorated rooms with harbor views, eat delicious breakfasts made with locally sourced ingredients, and visit the village's shops, pubs, and traditional music performances.

b. Oldchurch House, County Wicklow: Oldchurch House, a historic bed and breakfast in the village of Donard in County Wicklow, offers a peaceful escape to the countryside. Relax in elegant rooms with period features, eat homemade breakfasts in the charming dining room, and discover the scenic beauty of the Wicklow Mountains and Glendalough Valley.

**Historic Hospitality**

a. Rocklands House Bed and Breakfast, County Wexford: Immerse yourself in history at Rocklands House Bed and Breakfast, a Georgian farmhouse from the 18th century in County Wexford. Stay in comfortable rooms with antique furnishings, eat delicious breakfasts made with farm-fresh produce, and visit the historic sites and beautiful beaches of Ireland's Sunny Southeast.

b. Kilmokea Country Manor, County Wexford: Kilmokea Country Manor is a charming bed and breakfast located in a historic Georgian manor house surrounded by lush gardens in County Wexford. Relax in elegant rooms with period details, take a stroll through the gardens and woodland trails, and unwind in the indoor pool and sauna for a truly luxurious and unforgettable stay.

Budget-Friendly Hostels and Camping

**Hostel Havens**

a. Barnacles Hostel in Dublin: Barnacles Hostel, located in the heart of Temple Bar, provides a budget-friendly way to experience Dublin's vibrant atmosphere. Stay in a dormitory or private room, get free breakfast and Wi-Fi, and take advantage of the hostel's central location to visit Dublin's top attractions, nightlife, and cultural sites.

b. Kinlay Hostel, Galway: Discover the charm of Galway City at Kinlay Hostel, which is just steps away from Eyre Square and Galway's bustling Latin Quarter. Stay in a comfortable dormitory or private room, unwind in the welcoming common areas, and participate in the hostel's social events and activities, such as pub crawls and live music performances.

**Camping Adventures**

a. Glen of Aherlow Caravan and Camping Park in County Tipperary: Located in County Tipperary's scenic Glen of Aherlow, this park offers a peaceful escape to nature. Pitch your tent or park your caravan amidst lush greenery, take in breathtaking views of the surrounding mountains, and explore the area's hiking trails, waterfalls, and historic sites.

b. Roundwood Caravan and Camping Park, County Wicklow: Enjoy the beauty of the Wicklow Mountains at Roundwood Caravan and Camping Park, which is located near the charming village of Roundwood. Set up camp in a peaceful woodland setting, enjoy outdoor activities like hiking, fishing, and cycling, and visit nearby attractions such as Glendalough and Powerscourt Estate.

**Coastal Retreats**

a. Neptune's Hostel in Killorglin, County Kerry: This facility offers a coastal retreat to explore Ireland's southwest coast. Stay in a low-cost dormitory or private room, unwind in the hostel's communal lounge and kitchen, and discover the breathtaking Ring of Kerry, Dingle Peninsula, and Killarney National Park.

b. Strandhill Caravan and Camping Park, County Sligo: Enjoy the surf culture of Ireland's west coast at Strandhill Caravan and Camping Park, which is just steps from the beach in County Sligo. Set up camp in the dunes overlooking the Atlantic Ocean, enjoy beach activities like surfing and kiteboarding, and soak up the laid-back vibe of this coastal community.

**Rural Retreats**

a. Black Valley Hostel in County Kerry: Experience the rugged beauty of Ireland's remote countryside at Black Valley Hostel, which is located in the heart of the Black Valley in County Kerry. Stay in basic dormitory rooms, eat homemade meals prepared by your hosts, and explore the surrounding hiking trails, lakes, and mountains for a true wilderness adventure.

b. Ben Lettery Connemara Hostel, County Galway: Discover the wild beauty of Connemara at Ben Lettery Connemara Hostel, which is located in the heart of Connemara's Twelve Bens mountain range in County Galway. Stay in a rustic dormitory or private room, take in the panoramic views of the mountains and lakes, and discover the area's hiking trails, scenic drives, and traditional villages.

# FOOD AND DRINK

Traditional Irish Dishes to Try

**Hearty Classics**

a. Irish Stew: Dig into a bowl of hearty Irish stew, a comforting dish made with tender lamb or beef, potatoes, onions, carrots, and herbs. Enjoy the rich flavors and hearty textures of this classic Irish comfort food, ideal for warming up on a cold day.

b. Boxty: Enjoy the delicious simplicity of boxty, a traditional Irish potato pancake made from grated potatoes, flour, baking powder, and buttermilk. Boxty can be served as a side dish or as a main course, with toppings like bacon, eggs, or smoked salmon for a complete meal.

**Seafood Specialties**

a. Dublin Bay Prawn Cocktail: Experience luxury with succulent prawns served in a tangy cocktail sauce, crisp lettuce, and lemon wedges. Enjoy this traditional seafood dish as a starter or light meal served with freshly baked Irish soda bread.

b. Galway Oysters: Try the freshest Galway oysters, harvested from the pristine waters of Galway Bay, and enjoy the briny sweetness and delicate texture of these famous bivalves. Enjoy freshly shucked oysters served on the half shell, with a squeeze of lemon or a dash of mignonette sauce for extra flavor.

**Savory Pies and Pastries**

a. Beef and Guinness Pie: Savor the rich and hearty flavors of beef and Guinness pie, a traditional Irish dish that features tender beef stewed in rich Guinness gravy, topped with flaky pastry, and baked until golden brown. Enjoy the savory goodness of this comforting pie with a side of mashed potatoes or buttered vegetables.

b. Traditional Irish Soda Bread: Enjoy the simplicity of traditional Irish soda bread, a rustic loaf made from flour, baking soda, salt, and buttermilk that is baked until golden brown. Slices of soda bread slathered in creamy butter or topped with Irish smoked salmon and a sprinkle of fresh dill make a delicious snack or accompaniment to soups and stews.

**Sweet Treats**

a. Irish Apple Cake: Treat your sweet tooth with this moist and flavorful cake made with tart apples, warm spices, and a hint of brown sugar. Enjoy this traditional Irish dessert on its own or with whipped cream or vanilla ice cream for a delectable treat.

b. Baileys Irish Cream Cheesecake: Indulge in a decadent slice of Baileys Irish Cream Cheesecake, which has a rich and creamy cheesecake filling infused with the flavors of Baileys Irish Cream Liqueur and is nestled on a buttery graham cracker crust. Enjoy every indulgent bite of this luxurious dessert, which is topped with a drizzle of chocolate ganache or a sprinkle of cocoa powder for added decadence.

## The Craft Beer and Whiskey Scene

**Craft Beer Pubs**

a. The Porterhouse Brewing Company, Dublin: Immerse yourself in Dublin's craft beer scene by visiting The Porterhouse Brewing Company, a pioneering brewery and pub in Temple Bar. Sample a variety of handcrafted beers brewed on-site, including stouts, ales, and lagers, while enjoying the lively atmosphere of this iconic Dublin pub.

b. Galway Bay Brewery in Galway: Galway Bay Brewery, a well-known brewery and pub with locations throughout the city, offers an opportunity to immerse yourself in Galway's vibrant craft beer culture. Enjoy a wide range of innovative and flavorful beers, from hoppy IPAs to rich stouts, and unwind in the welcoming pubs, which frequently host live music and events.

**Whiskey Distilleries**

a. Jameson Distillery, Bow St., Dublin: Discover the rich history and heritage of Irish whiskey at the Jameson Distillery Bow St. in Dublin, Jameson whiskey's original home. Take a guided tour of the historic distillery, learn about the whiskey-making process from grain to glass, and sample some of Jameson's signature blends and limited-edition releases.

b. Midleton Distillery, County Cork: Visit the Midleton Distillery in County Cork, which produces some of Ireland's most iconic whiskey brands, including Jameson, Redbreast, and Powers. Take a behind-the-scenes tour of the cutting-edge distillery, explore the expansive warehouses where whiskey is aged to perfection, and enjoy guided tastings of premium Irish whiskeys.

**Hidden Wine Gems**

a. The Burren Brewery in County Clare: This is a small craft brewery surrounded by scenic landscapes. Enjoy guided brewery tours and tastings of their unique and flavorful beers, which are inspired by the rugged beauty of the Burren region.

b. Teeling Distillery, Dublin: Teeling Distillery, a boutique distillery in Dublin's historic Liberties neighborhood, is reviving the city's whiskey-making traditions. Take a guided tour of the distillery, learn about Teeling's innovative whiskey production process, and sample their award-winning small-batch and single malt whiskeys.

**Cultural Experiences**

a. Whiskey Tasting at Dick Mack's in County Kerry. Dick Mack's, a legendary pub and whiskey bar in the picturesque town of Dingle, County Kerry, offers an immersion in Irish whiskey culture. Attend whiskey tastings led by knowledgeable staff, browse their extensive collection of rare and vintage whiskeys, and enjoy the warm hospitality and convivial atmosphere of this iconic Irish pub.

b. Beer Gardens at The Bernard Shaw, Dublin: The Bernard Shaw, a trendy pub and cultural hub in Dublin's vibrant Portobello neighborhood, captures the laid-back vibe of the city's hipster scene. Relax in the beer garden, which is adorned with street art and graffiti.

## SAFETY AND ETIQUETTE

Navigating Ireland Safely

**Transportation Tips**

When driving in Ireland, follow local traffic laws and regulations, which include driving on the left side of the road. Be cautious on narrow country lanes and rural roads, and be aware of pedestrians, cyclists, and livestock that may be sharing the road.

Use buses, trains, and trams to travel between cities and towns conveniently and cost-effectively. Familiarize yourself with schedules, routes, and ticketing options, and be prepared for crowded conditions during peak travel periods.

To ensure outdoor safety, be aware of weather conditions and forecasts before engaging in activities like hiking, cycling, or water sports. Prepare for sudden weather changes, such as rain, wind, and fog, and dress appropriately with layers and waterproof clothing.

Be cautious when exploring Ireland's rugged landscapes and natural attractions, such as coastal cliffs, mountains, and national parks. Stay on designated trails, follow safety guidelines, and avoid risky activities like climbing on unstable terrain or swimming in dangerous waters.

Protect your personal belongings and valuables while traveling in Ireland, especially in busy tourist areas and public transportation hubs. Keep your belongings secure and be wary of pickpocketing and theft, especially in urban areas and tourist hotspots.

Be familiar with emergency contact information, such as the local emergency services number (999 or 112) and the locations of hospitals, police stations, and embassies or consulates. Carry a fully charged phone and a basic first-aid kit in case of an emergency.

During your visit, please respect Irish customs, traditions, and cultural norms. Be mindful of local customs such as greetings, table manners, and social etiquette, and observe any religious or cultural practices with sensitivity and understanding.

Practice responsible tourism by reducing your environmental impact and protecting Ireland's natural resources and wildlife. Dispose of waste properly, adhere to Leave No Trace principles, and support environmentally friendly initiatives and conservation efforts.

## Health Services for Tourists

**Medical Facilities**

a. Hospitals and Clinics: Familiarize yourself with the locations of hospitals, clinics, and medical centers in the areas you intend to visit in Ireland. Major cities and tourist destinations usually have well-equipped hospitals with emergency rooms and specialized medical services.

b. Pharmacies: Look up nearby pharmacies where you can buy over-the-counter medications, prescription drugs, and medical supplies. In Ireland, pharmacists can provide advice on minor ailments as well as information on local healthcare services.

**Emergency Services**

a. Emergency Medical Services: In the event of a medical emergency, call the national emergency number (999 or 112) for immediate assistance. Emergency medical services in Ireland are ready to respond to a variety of medical emergencies and can send ambulances and medical personnel to your location.

b. Travel Insurance: Consider purchasing travel insurance that covers medical emergencies, hospitalization, and repatriation in case of illness or injury during your trip to Ireland. Verify the scope of coverage and become acquainted with the procedures for seeking medical treatment and filing insurance claims.

**Vaccination and Health Precautions**

a. Routine Vaccinations: Before traveling to Ireland, make sure all of your routine vaccinations are up to date. Measles, mumps, rubella (MMR), influenza, and tetanus-diphtheria-pertussis (Tdap) are some of the vaccinations that are recommended.

b. Health Precautions: To avoid illness during your trip, practice good hygiene, drink bottled or boiled water, and avoid eating or drinking from questionable sources. If you have any specific health concerns or dietary restrictions, make them known to healthcare providers and accommodation providers in advance.

**Travel Health Resources**

a. Health Information: To stay informed about health-related issues in Ireland, consult reliable sources like the World Health Organization (WHO), the Centers for Disease Control and Prevention (CDC), and the Health Service Executive (HSE).

b. Medical Assistance for Visitors: Seek non-emergency medical attention at local clinics or general practitioners (GPs) in Ireland. Some clinics may accept walk-in appointments from tourists, while others may require prior booking or a referral from a healthcare provider.

## PLANNING YOUR DEPARTURE

Souvenirs and Memories to Bring Back Home

**Traditional Irish Crafts**

a. Aran Sweaters: Handcrafted from soft wool with intricate cable knit patterns, these sweaters provide warmth and comfort. Choose from a variety of styles and colors to suit your preferences, and bring home a timeless piece of Irish craftsmanship.

b. Connemara Marble: Admire the natural beauty of Connemara marble, a rare and distinctive stone found exclusively in Ireland's Connemara region. Choose from a variety of handmade jewelry, home decor items, and souvenirs made from this distinctive green marble, and keep a piece of Ireland's geological heritage.

## Celtic Keepsakes

a. Claddagh Ring: The Claddagh ring, which represents love, loyalty, and friendship, is a beloved Irish tradition that dates back more than 300 years. Choose from a variety of Claddagh rings made of sterling silver, gold, or platinum, and wear this timeless symbol of Irish heritage with pride.

b. Celtic Knotwork: Explore the intricate beauty of Celtic knotwork, an ancient art form distinguished by interlocking patterns and symbolism. Bring home a piece of Celtic knotwork jewelry, artwork, or home decor to fill your home with the rich history and symbolism of Ireland's Celtic heritage.

## Culinary Delights

a. Irish Whiskey. Indulge in the smooth and complex flavors of Irish whiskey, which is known for its high quality and craftsmanship. Choose from a variety of premium Irish whiskey brands and expressions to experience the distinct flavor of Ireland's signature spirit.

b. Irish Cheese and Chocolate: Indulge your taste buds with the rich and creamy flavors of Irish cheese and chocolate, made from the best local ingredients and traditional recipes. Choose from a selection of artisanal cheeses, chocolate truffles, and confections to bring a taste of Ireland's culinary delights to your home.

**Artisanal Crafts**

a. Handmade Pottery: Discover the beauty of Irish craftsmanship with handmade pottery made by skilled artisans using traditional techniques. Choose from a variety of pottery items, including mugs, bowls, and vases, each reflecting the distinctive style and creativity of Ireland's potters.

b. Wool and Textiles: Enjoy the luxurious softness and warmth of Irish wool and textiles, which are woven into a variety of blankets, scarves, and throws. Choose from a palette of natural colors and patterns inspired by Ireland's landscapes and heritage, and bring home a warm reminder of your visit to the Emerald Isle.

Reflecting on Your Journey

Reflect on your immersive experiences in Ireland, including exploring historic landmarks and natural wonders, connecting with locals, and embracing Irish culture. Recall your feelings of awe and wonder as you discover the beauty and diversity of the Emerald Isle.

Think about the cultural connections you've formed during your time in Ireland, whether through shared stories and traditions, lively music and dance, or warm hospitality and friendship. Keep the memories of meaningful interactions and authentic experiences that have helped you understand Irish life and heritage.

Review photos and memories from your Ireland trip to relive the sights, sounds, and sensations. From breathtaking landscapes and historic sites to vibrant festivals and bustling markets, each photograph tells a story and captures a treasured memory of your journey.

Look back on your trip to Ireland through the pages of your travel journal, where you documented your thoughts, observations, and emotions along the way. Relive the moments of inspiration, introspection, and discovery that shaped your narrative of Ireland and left an indelible mark on your heart.

Reflect on the cultural insights and lessons you learned while in Ireland, developing a greater appreciation for the country's history, traditions, and values. Consider the diversity and complexities of Irish identity, as well as how your experiences have broadened and enriched your worldview.

Consider the personal growth and transformation that occurred during your journey through Ireland, as you navigated new experiences, overcame obstacles, and formed connections with others. Celebrate the fortitude, curiosity, and open-mindedness that have led you on this transformative journey.

Say goodbye to the Emerald Isle, leaving a piece of your heart and carrying cherished memories and experiences that will last a lifetime. As you leave Ireland, keep the spirit of the country with you and remember that you are always welcome to return to its shores with open arms.

# IRELAND ITINERARIES

Weekend Getaway (2-3 Days)

**Day 1: Dublin Exploration**

Explore Dublin's historic landmarks, including Trinity College, Dublin Castle, and St. Patrick's Cathedral.

Explore the vibrant streets of Temple Bar, stopping by shops, galleries, and cafes.

Visit the Guinness Storehouse for a tour and a taste of Ireland's famous stout.

In a lively Dublin pub, you can spend the evening listening to traditional music and eating pub food.

**Day 2: Coastal Excursion**

Explore County Wicklow, also known as the "Garden of Ireland," with a drive or day tour along its stunning coastline.

Explore the picturesque village of Glendalough, including its ancient monastic site and scenic hiking trails.

Visit Powerscourt Estate to admire the beautiful gardens and historic mansion.

Return to Dublin for a farewell dinner at a local restaurant, enjoying Irish cuisine and hospitality.

## Weeklong Adventure (6-7 days)

### Day 1-2: Dublin and its Surroundings

Spend the first day exploring Dublin's highlights, as detailed in the Weekend Getaway itinerary.

On day two, leave Dublin and visit nearby attractions like Malahide Castle, Howth Peninsula, and the Newgrange Passage Tomb.

Return to Dublin for another night, or continue to your next destination.

### Day 3–4: Galway and Connemara

Travel west to the vibrant city of Galway, which is known for its lively atmosphere and traditional music scene.

Explore Galway's charming streets, colorful shops, and historic sites such as Eyre Square and Galway Cathedral.

Take a day trip to Connemara National Park to hike scenic trails, visit Kylemore Abbey, and appreciate the rugged beauty of the region.

Return to Galway for a night of live music and craic at a nearby pub.

### Day 5–6: County Clare and the Cliffs of Moher

Travel south to County Clare to see the iconic Cliffs of Moher, one of Ireland's most stunning natural wonders.

Explore the quaint village of Doolin, known for its traditional music pubs and proximity to the cliffs.

Take a scenic drive along the Wild Atlantic Way, stopping at scenic viewpoints and coastal towns such as Lahinch and Kilkee.

Spend your final evening in County Clare with a seafood dinner overlooking the Atlantic Ocean.

## Two Weeks of Exploration

### Day 1–3: Dublin and East Coast

Begin your journey in Dublin and spend a few days exploring the city's attractions and nearby sights, as detailed in the Weekend Getaway itinerary.

### Day 4–6: Northern Ireland

Cross the border into Northern Ireland and visit Belfast, where you can see the Titanic Belfast museum, political murals, and the Giant's Causeway.

Spend the day exploring the scenic Antrim Coast, visiting attractions such as Carrick-a-Rede Rope Bridge and Dunluce Castle.

Return to Dublin, or continue south to your next destination.

### Day 7-10: Southern Ireland- Cork and Kerry

Travel south to County Cork to discover the city of Cork, the historic port town of Cobh, and the breathtaking scenery of West Cork.

Travel west to County Kerry to discover the Ring of Kerry, Killarney National Park, and the Dingle Peninsula.

Take some time to hike, bike, or simply enjoy the breathtaking scenery along Ireland's southwest coast.

### Day 11–14: West Coast and Connemara

Travel north along the Wild Atlantic Way to County Clare to see the Cliffs of Moher, the Burren, and the charming villages of Doolin and Kinvara.

Continue your journey to Galway and spend the day exploring the city and the nearby Connemara National Park.

On your final day, return to Dublin or extend your stay to see more of Ireland's capital city.

# APPENDICES

Useful Phrases in Irish

### 1. Greetings and Basics

Hello: Dia dhuit (pronounced "dee-ah-gwitch")

Goodbye: Slán (pronounced "Slawn")

Thank you! Go raibh maith agat! (pronounced: "guh rev mah agut")

Please: Más é do thoilé (pronounced "maws ay duh hull ay").

Excuse me: Gabh mo leithscéal, pronounced "gahv muh lesh-kayl"

### 2. Conversation Starters

How are you doing? Conas atá tú? (pronounced "Kun-iss ah-taw too")

What's your name? Is Cad ainm Duit? (pronounced "Kahd iss an-im gwitch")

My name is: Is mise. (pronounced: "iss mish-eh")

Where are you from? What are your plans for today? (pronounced "Kah will too Ih duh khoh-nee")

## 3. Directions & Travel

Where is...?: Ca bhfuil...? (pronounced "Kah Will")

How to get there: Conas a fháil go dtí...? (pronounced "Kun-iss Ah Faw-il Goh Dee")

I am lost. Tá mé caillte, pronounced "taw may kahl-cheh"

Can you help me? Do you have any questions? (pronounced "Ahn Fay-dir Lat kow-roo lum")

## 4. Dining Out

I would like...: Ba mhaith liom (pronounced "bah wah lum")

Menu: Méinéar (pronounced "may-near").

Water: Uisce, pronounced "ish-keh"

Bill, please: An bille, más é do thoilé (pronounced "ahn bill-eh, maws ay duh hull ay").

## 5. Emergency

Help! Cabhair! (pronounced, "kah-wir")

I need a doctor. Tá de dhochtúir uaim, pronounced "taw day duck-tore ooh-ihm"

Call the police: Glaoigh ar na póilíní, pronounced "glwee air na poy-lee-nee"

Where is the nearest hospital: Cá bhfuil an ospidéal cóngarach? (pronounced "Kah Will on ush-pee-dawl iss koh-ngur-ah")

## 6. Common Expressions

Yes: Tá, pronounced "taw"

No: Níl, pronounced "neel"

Sorry: Tá Brón Orm (pronounced "taw Brohn Or-um")

I do not understand: Ní Thuigim (pronounced "nee Hwig-im")

Cheers!: Sláinte! (pronounced: "slawn-chuh")

## 7. Farewell

Goodbye: Slán leat, pronounced "slawn lat"

See you later: Slán go fóill, pronounced "slawn guh foy-ill"

Until we meet again: Go mbeirimid beo ar an am seo arís, pronounced "guh may-rih-mid byoh er on am shuh a-reesh".

Useful Contacts and Resources

Useful Contacts and Useful Contacts and Resources

**1. Emergency Services**

Police (Gardaí): 999 or 112.

Ambulance: 999 or 112.

Fire Department: 999 or 112

**2. Health Services**

Health Service Executive (HSE): +353 1 635 4000.

Hospitals and clinics: For medical assistance, contact local hospital or clinic.

**3. Tourist Information**

Failte Ireland (the National Tourism Development Authority): +353 1 884 7700.

Local Tourist Information Offices: For maps, brochures, and travel advice, go to your local tourist information office.

**4. Transport Services**

Irish Rail (Train Services): +353 1 836 6222.

Bus Éireann (Bus Service): +353 1 836 6111.

Dublin Bus (Dublin City Bus Services): +353 1 873 4222.

Irish Ferries (Ferry Services): +353 818 300 400.

## 5. Embassy and Consulate Contacts

Embassy of Your Country in Ireland: Contact your country's embassy or consulate for help and support.

Contact the Department of Foreign Affairs and Trade (Ireland) at +353 1 408 2000.

## 6. Travel Insurance Providers

Contact your travel insurance company for help with medical emergencies, trip cancellations, and other travel-related issues.

## 7. Language Resources

Learn basic Irish phrases and language skills using the Duolingo app or website.

Enroll in Irish language classes or workshops at your local community center or language school.

## 8. Outdoor Adventure Guides

Mountaineering Ireland: +353 1 625 1115.

Cycling Ireland: +353 1 855 1522.

Irish Surfing Association: +353 87 652 1386.

**9. Tour Operators and Guides**

Discover local tour operators and guides who offer guided tours, outdoor adventures, and cultural experiences.

**10. Local authorities**

For information on local weather, road closures, and other issues, contact the appropriate authorities.

Save these contacts and resources for easy access while traveling in Ireland. Whether you require emergency assistance, travel advice, or language assistance, these resources can help you have a safe and enjoyable trip to Ireland.

Irish Festivals Calendar

**1. St. Patrick's Day, March 17th**

Location: Nationwide, with major celebrations in Dublin, Cork, and Galway.

Ireland's national holiday is marked by parades, music, dance, and cultural events honoring the patron saint of Ireland.

**2. Galway International Arts Festival, July**

Location: Galway City, County Galway

A two-week arts festival featuring theater performances, music concerts, visual arts exhibitions, street performances, and other activities.

**3. Electric Picnic, September**

Location: Stradbally, County Laois.

Ireland's largest music and arts festival, with a diverse lineup of musical acts, comedy shows, art installations, and interactive activities.

**4. Dublin Fringe Festival, September**

Location: Dublin City, County Dublin.

A multidisciplinary arts festival that features innovative and experimental performances in theater, dance, music, comedy, and visual arts.

**5. Dublin International Film Festival, February-March**

Location: Dublin City, County Dublin.

An international film festival featuring screenings, premieres, panel discussions, and special events with filmmakers and industry professionals.

6. Cork Jazz Festival, October

Location: Cork City, County Cork.

A vibrant celebration of jazz music featuring live performances by local and international artists, jazz workshops, masterclasses, and jam sessions at various venues throughout the city.

**7. Lisdoonvarna Matchmaking Festival, August to September**

Location: Lisdoonvarna, County Clare.

Europe's largest singles event, with traditional Irish music, dancing, and matchmaking activities for singles looking for love and romance.

**8. Fleadh Cheoil Na hÉireann, August**

Location: Various host towns in Ireland.

The world's largest traditional Irish music festival, with competitions, concerts, workshops, and sessions celebrating Irish music, song, and dance.

**9. National Ploughing Championships, September**

Tullamore, County Offaly (changes annually).

Europe's largest outdoor agricultural event, featuring plowing competitions, livestock displays, trade exhibits, food stalls, and family-friendly entertainment.

**10. Galway Oyster Festival, September**

Location: Galway City, County Galway.

An oyster and seafood festival featuring oyster shucking competitions, gourmet food tastings, live music, and cultural events that highlight Galway's culinary heritage.

Travel Checklist

**1. Travel Documents**

Passport and visa (if applicable).

Travel Insurance Documents

Itinerary and reservation confirmations

Driver's license (if renting a vehicle)

Emergency contact information

**2. Money and Banking**

Local currency (Euro in Ireland)

Credit, debit, and ATM cards

Traveler's checks, if desired.

Contact details for your bank

Currency conversion app or calculator.

### 3. Health and Safety

Prescription medications and prescription copies.

Pain relievers, antihistamines, and other OTC medications

First Aid Kit

Travel health insurance information

Hand sanitizer, disinfectant wipes

Face masks and personal protective equipment.

### 4. Electronics and Gadgets

Smartphone and charger.

Travel adapter and voltage converter (if necessary)

Camera or smartphone to capture memories

Portable power banks

Headphones or Earbuds

Laptop or tablet (optional).

### 5. Clothing & Accessories

Weather-appropriate clothing (layers for changing weather)

Comfortable walking shoes.

Raincoat or umbrella

Sunscreen and sunglasses.

Hat or cap

Swimsuit and towel (when visiting beaches or pools)

### 6. Travel gear

Luggage (a suitcase, backpack, or duffle bag)

Daypack or tote bag for daily outings.

Travel locks and baggage tags

Travel pillows and blankets

Travel guides and maps

Portable luggage scale (to check baggage weight)

### 7. Toiletries and Personal Care

Toothbrush, toothpaste, and dental floss.

Shampoo, Conditioner, and Body Wash

Hair brush or comb

Razor and shaving cream.

feminine hygiene products.

Personal hygiene products (hand sanitizer, wet wipes, tissues)

**8. Miscellaneous Items**

Travel journal and pen.

Reading materials or e-readers

Snack and water bottle

Reusable shopping bags

Travel-sized laundry detergent (for handwashing clothes).

Entertainment (cards, travel games)

**9. Important Contacts**

Emergency contacts (local emergency services, embassy, or consulate)

Contact information for accommodations and tour operators.

Contact information for friends and family back home.

Phone numbers and addresses for local services (hospitals, police stations, pharmacies)

## 10. Others

Any items or equipment specific to your activities or interests (hiking gear, snorkeling equipment, etc.)

Keep a travel journal or notebook to record memories and experiences

International driving permit (if you intend to rent a car).

Language phrasebook or translation application

Printed in Great Britain
by Amazon